*M*ORE THAN
PETTICOAT*S*

REMARKABLE
NEW YORK *W*OMEN

MORE THAN PETTICOATS

REMARKABLE NEW YORK WOMEN

Antonia Petrash

TWODOT®

Guilford, Connecticut
An imprint of The Globe Pequot Press

A · T W O D O T ® · B O O K

Cover photo courtesy of the Robert R. Coles Long Island History Collection at the Glen Cove Public Library, Glen Cove, New York.

Library of Congress Cataloging-in-Publication Data
Petrash, Antonia.
   More than petticoats : remarkable New York women / Antonia Petrash.— 1st ed.
     p. cm. — (More than petticoats series)
   Includes bibliographical references and index.
   Contents: Deborah Dunch Moody, a dangerous woman — Kateri Tekakwitha, the lily of the Mohawks — Sybil Ludington, the female Paul Revere — Emma Hart Willard, champion of education for women — Amelia Jenks Bloomer, the well-dressed suffragist — Harriet Tubman, the Moses of her people — Emily Warren Roebling, an unlikely bridge builder — Katharine Bement Davis, prison reformer — Mary Burnett Talbert, advocate of equality — Sara Josephine Baker, champion of health care for children — Gertrude Vanderbilt Whitney, patron of American art — Dorothy Day, founder of the Catholic Worker Movement.
   ISBN 0-7627-1223-6
   1. Women—New York (State)—Biography. 2. Women—New York (State)—History. 3. New York (State)—Biography. I. Title: Remarkable New York women. II. Title. III. Series.

CT3260 .P48 2002
920.72'09747—dc21

                                               2001045045

♻ Text printed on recycled paper
Manufactured in the United States of America
First Edition/First Printing

CONTENTS

ACKNOWLEDGMENTS
vii

INTRODUCTION
ix

DEBORAH DUNCH MOODY
A Dangerous Woman
1

KATERI TEKAKWITHA
The Lily of the Mohawks
13

SYBIL LUDINGTON
The Female Paul Revere
25

EMMA HART WILLARD
Champion of Education for Women
35

AMELIA JENKS BLOOMER
The Well-Dressed Suffragist
48

HARRIET TUBMAN
The Moses of Her People
62

EMILY WARREN ROEBLING
An Unlikely Bridge Builder
76

KATHARINE BEMENT DAVIS
Prison Reformer
90

MARY BURNETT TALBERT
Advocate of Equality
103

SARA JOSEPHINE BAKER
Champion of Health Care for Children
116

GERTRUDE VANDERBILT WHITNEY
Patron of American Art
130

DOROTHY DAY
Founder of the Catholic Worker Movement
143

BIBLIOGRAPHY
159

INDEX
167

$\mathscr{A}$CKNOWLEDGMENTS

$\mathscr{N}$o one writes a book in a vacuum, certainly not one that takes such extensive research. Sincere thanks go to Christopher Densmore of the University of Buffalo Archives; to Edward G. Schwaegerle of the Oberlin College Archives; to librarians at the Frances Mulhall Achilles Library and Archives of the Whitney Museum of American Art; to Joy Holland of the Brooklyn Public Library; to the active members of the Catholic Worker Movement who shared their current publications and their goals with me; to author Vincent Dacquinto, who first brought Sybil Ludington's story to life; to John Fox and Christina Mucciolo of the Putnam Valley Historical Society; to George M. Sands of the Freedom Trail Project of New York State; and to Thomas C. McCarthy of the New York City Bureau of Corrections.

I am especially indebted to all my supportive friends who offered wonderful suggestions and who seemed to never tire of hearing about the book; to the members of the Saturday morning Nonfiction Writers Group at the Glen Cove Public Library; and to all my friends and co-workers at the Glen Cove Public Library, especially interloan clerk Amy Mondello, whose cheerful handling of dozens of requests made the research so much easier.

I would also like to thank my editor, Charlene Patterson, for her thoughtful and insightful suggestions; my daughters and sisters and their families for their loving support; and especially my husband, Jack, without whose unflagging devotion and encouragement this work would not have been possible.

ℐNTRODUCTION

"ℐf only they had done as they were told." As I researched and wrote the stories of the women in this book that thought occurred to me again and again. If these twelve women, and others like them, had adhered to the expectations that society had set for them—had only just listened to the "voices of reason" of their day—there would be no need for this book at all, and life as we know it might be very different. There would be few women in the professions, few taking an active role in politics, fewer still owning and managing their own property.

From the beginning of civilization as we know it, women were told to stay within the confines of hearth and home and leave the rest of the business of life to men. They were supposed to hide their true natures behind the self-respecting veneer of family life, when perhaps they really wanted to become artists, doctors, writers, political activists, or educators. One size was supposed to fit all women, and all women were supposed to be happy with the fit.

But the women in this book, and others like them, did not listen to those "voices of reason." They knew that one size did not fit all. They longed to be more than just wives and mothers, as respectable and as laudable as those life choices might be. They longed to join professions, study advanced subjects, found settlements, enjoy religious freedom, protest any and all inequalities, and even join the battles of war. Such longings were considered to be at best gauche, at least grounds for ridicule and exile. Unmarried women had few professional choices beyond teaching and often faced lives of abject poverty. Before the Women's Property Act of 1850, in New York married women had no claim to their own property, to their own wages, even to the custody of their own children.

The impetus for change was especially strong among New York women. Indeed, the women's rights movement itself was officially born in New York in 1848 in the small and unassuming village of Seneca Falls. Coming from sophisticated city streets and humble rural lanes, these New York women who would not do as they were told joined their voices with women in other states, and eventually a persistent clamor rose that could not be ignored. Speeches were made; newspapers were published and books were written. These speeches and writings, combined with marches and demonstrations, would eventually form a powerful river of protest that still flows to this day.

Some of the women in this book chose not to demonstrate but to quietly strive to change society from the inside out. Of necessity I limited the women to be featured here to those born before 1900, and one of the difficulties I encountered in my search for remarkable New York women was limiting the number to twelve. There are literally hundreds of others whose stories are equally compelling. And as my twelve women broke from tradition, their paths crossed and crossed again, weaving an invisible web of support that the women themselves were sometimes unaware of but ultimately benefited from. Harriet Tubman did not know Amelia Jenks Bloomer, but she did notice the new fashion of trousers that Amelia wore and adopted them because they were practical and comfortable. Katharine Bement Davis wrote to Mary Burnett Talbert to offer support to her actions against the lynching of African Americans. Mary Burnett Talbert visited Harriet Tubman in her old age to honor her work of leading slaves to freedom. Emma Hart Willard and Sara Josephine Baker were raised along the same banks of the Hudson River as Emily Warren Roebling.

Most of these women enjoyed a happy childhood in a family where education for girls was prized, which was fortuitous, education being one of the main keys to progress. Most came from families of moderate means, but some were poor and at least one was wealthy beyond imagining. All envisioned a different world than the one they inhabited. All shared an amazing bravery of spirit that urged them to go beyond the narrow expectations of their sex and their time. The steps they took forged a path to freedom and equality that others would follow—a path that would eventually lead to the rights and freedoms women enjoy today. I felt both humbled by their accomplishments and honored to research and write about their lives.

And if they had only done as they were told, none of it would have ever happened.

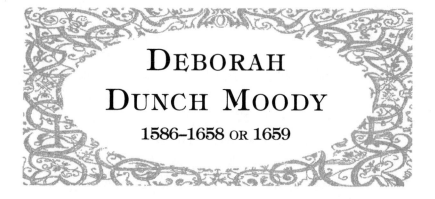

DEBORAH DUNCH MOODY

1586–1658 OR 1659

A Dangerous Woman

*T*he small ship rose and fell with the buffeting waves, lashed by the cold winds of the wild Atlantic. The travelers onboard were a frightened but determined lot, and none was more determined than the gentle but strong-willed aristocrat, Lady Deborah Moody. Deborah Dunch Moody had left her comfortable home in England and traveled halfway across the world to seek nothing less than the elusive rights of religious and political freedom. But first, she had to survive the perilous and seemingly endless journey.

She made the voyage around 1638, traveling not with immediate family members but with friends from England who shared her Anabaptist faith. Leaving the only life they had ever known, they braved untried sea captains, wild storms, brazen pirates, and the challenge of a new land simply because the government in England denied them the freedom to worship God as they chose. After several months at sea, they finally reached the settlement of Boston in Massachusetts. For the average family traveling together, it had been a frightening and dangerous journey. For a middle-aged woman traveling alone, it had been an act of utmost bravery and daring.

But it would not be the last brave and daring act Lady Deborah Moody would perform. Before long she would travel to still other unknown ports and do battle with intolerant religious fanatics and native tribes. She would be the first woman to be granted a land patent in the American colonies. The settlement she founded would be one of the first to allow its inhabitants to worship God as they pleased. And, as if that was not enough, she would be the first woman known to cast a vote in her adopted land.

Deborah Dunch was born in 1586 in Wiltshire, England, the eldest daughter of Walter and Debora Dunch. Her father was a member of Parliament. Her mother's father was James Pilkington, a Protestant bishop who often spoke against religious intolerance. Most of Deborah's childhood was spent at the peaceful and prosperous family estate in Wiltshire in the English countryside. There, Deborah and her sisters and brother were free to wander through the fields of the 3,000-acre farm, where sheep grazed and crops grew in abundance.

The Dunch children enjoyed the privileges of wealth and title, including a comprehensive education available only to the rich. Although women were not allowed to attend a university and education was generally believed to be wasted on girls, Deborah and her three sisters learned to read and were encouraged to develop social graces that the family hoped would ultimately result in successful marriage contracts. Deborah was eight years old when her father died in 1594, but her mother remarried four years later to another member of Parliament, Sir James Marvyn, and Deborah's life continued much as it had before.

But outside the walls of the family's country estate, life was anything but serene. A Catholic queen, Mary Queen of Scots, a claimant to the English throne, had been executed when Deborah was three months old. A Protestant, Queen Elizabeth I, ruled England, but Protestants still feared a return of Catholicism and religious persecution. When Deborah was seventeen, King James VI of Scotland was crowned James I, King of Great Britain, France, and Ireland. King James's reign would be marked by excessive religious and political intolerance, especially against Catholics and members of the Puritan sect. James believed in the divine right of kings, and worship that was contrary to *The Book of Common Prayer*, which contained the liturgy of the Church of England, was not allowed. There was no toleration of dissent; those who did not agree were quite often executed.

In 1606, at the age of twenty, Deborah married Henry Moody, who was knighted by King James soon after. Now she was Lady Deborah Moody, and she and her husband enjoyed a prosperous union that produced a son, Henry, in 1607, and a daughter, Catherina, in 1608. Sir Henry was named by King James as sheriff of Wiltshire in 1618, and in 1622 he was made a baronet. He did not enjoy these titles for long, however, for in 1629, at the age of forty-seven, he became ill on a trip to London and died soon after.

As a widow, Deborah was far from poor. The couple had amassed great wealth and owned several large estates and manor houses. But times were still turbulent. King James I had died, leaving his son Charles I to succeed him. Charles claimed even more royal rights and privileges than his father had, and he also vigorously continued his father's persecution of anyone who did not share his religious beliefs.

Deborah tried to stay above these conflicts, although she certainly did not agree with the teachings of the Church of England. She was particularly against the practice of infant baptism, believing that "children should not undergo important ceremonies until they were old enough to understand them." She kept these beliefs to herself, however, because that was the only way she could avoid persecution and continue to travel throughout the country as she wished.

But in June 1632 King Charles issued a royal proclamation limiting the amount of travel the gentry could enjoy. They were to stay at home in their country residences and were not to travel or reside in London. They were to quit spending money on "vaine delights and expences" and were commanded to invest their funds in their local communities.

Deborah felt this was an intolerable intrusion into her life. She was firm in her nonconformist beliefs and had many friends who felt the same way, particularly those of the Anabaptist faith, who agreed with her objection to infant baptism. She wanted to be free to visit these groups and to further explore different religious ideas, but the king's edict threatened to put an end to that. So in one of her most outspoken acts of dissent, she defied the court's command that she return from London to her country home of Garesdon, a defiance that finally drew the attention of the dreaded Star Chamber.

The Star Chamber was an English court of criminal and civil jurisdiction, seated at Westminster, and so called because of the painting of stars decorating the ceiling of the main room. Such a peaceful name belied its activities, however. The king had given the Star Chamber far-reaching powers, and its decisions were to be feared. The court ruled on such offenses as perjury, riot, libel, and conspiracy. Arbitrary punishments included imprisonment, whipping, and mutilation; the court stopped only at imposing the death penalty. Even jurors were vulnerable to the court's whims, because those who decided against the crown could be punished themselves.

England was Deborah's home. Her son lived nearby. Her daughter had been married in London in 1627. But when Lady Deborah learned of the Star Chamber's investigation into her activities, she realized that she was in danger, and that the wisest course for her to take was to leave England and immigrate to the New World.

The arrival of such a noble woman in Boston was exciting news. Deborah was warmly welcomed there by Governor John Winthrop. On May 13, 1640, the General Court granted her 400 acres of land for a plantation near the town of Lynn, Massachusetts, and in 1641 she purchased for the sum of 1,100 pounds a nearby estate called Swampscott from a fellow Englishman, Sir John Humphrey, who had decided to return to England. She also purchased a house in nearby Salem.

Grateful to find a new home at last, Deborah settled into the Salem community and joined the local church. But if she thought she would find religious freedom in Salem, she soon discovered she was mistaken. To her growing horror, Deborah discovered that the Puritans who had fled England to escape religious persecution were now inflicting even greater oppression on those who followed them to New England.

Believing that strict adherence to religious laws helped to develop a strong state, the Puritans passed arbitrary and severe laws that governed almost every aspect of the colonists' lives. Punishment was meted out for card playing, dancing, absence from church meetings, scolding, even kissing family members in public. Adultery by both men and women was subject to the death penalty. Women's behavior was even more stringently controlled than men's. Women were forbidden to wear certain styles of clothing, to cut their hair short, and, of course, to voice beliefs that differed with those of the clergy. In fact women had no voice in the community at all and were even forbidden to sing in church!

Deborah now faced another quandary. Her beliefs in freedom of worship had not changed, indeed had become more set; she was even more convinced of the validity of the Anabaptist faith, which reinforced her "radical" beliefs. Life in Salem was becoming increasingly intolerable. The stocks were crowded, with both men and women confined to them for long periods of time. The community whipping post was near Lady Deborah's house and was used often by the sheriff. She watched in horror while the community engaged in an active slave trade while preaching about the love of God.

The elders of the church questioned her frequently, insisting that she give up her Anabaptist leanings and adhere to their Puritan ways. Finally she was forced to admit that Salem was not a place that offered the freedom she sought. Again she decided the time had come to leave her home and seek a free life elsewhere.

Word spread quickly through the Salem community that Lady Deborah was leaving, and several families decided to go with her. It was known that some Anabaptists had journeyed to Long Island and had settled at Southampton. But Deborah knew that Holland had offered refuge to dissenters in Europe, so she hoped that the Dutch colony of New Amsterdam might offer the same refuge to her and her group. Fearing that during a journey over land they might possibly encounter hostile Indian tribes, the small group decided to go by sea.

Once again Deborah boarded a vessel, and once again she sailed out to sea, putting her life into the hands of an unknown sea captain. The vessel sailed around what is now Cape Cod, past Roger Williams's settlement in Rhode Island, and down through the Long Island Sound. It passed through the Narrows (now Throgs Neck), down the East River, and into New York Harbor.

In 1643 there was no Statue of Liberty in New York Harbor,

torch held high to greet emigrants. But Deborah Moody was a real "Lady Liberty," courageously seeking the same freedoms the statue would represent some 240 years later. Their journey finally over, the small group came ashore at New Amsterdam, the capital of what was then the Dutch settlement of New Netherlands.

They quickly discovered that New Amsterdam had problems of its own. Soon after landing they were forced to seek protection in a nearby fort from warring Mohican Indians. Deborah was weary of fighting and even briefly considered moving back to Massachusetts. But when news of her possible return reached New England, Governor Winthrop's deputy, John Endecott, discouraged the community's reacceptance of her. She had already been excommunicated by the Salem Church. A nervous Endecott wrote to Governor Winthrop, "I shall desire that she may not have advice to return to this jurisdiction, unless she will acknowledge her ewill [evil] in opposing the churches, and leave her opinions behinde her, for shee is a dangerous woeman."

Lady Deborah Moody had run as far as she could go. There was nowhere she could return to, no home waiting for her. She was fifty-seven years old, considered then to be the beginning of old age. But life for the determined traveler was finally about to take a turn for the better.

The settlement of New Amsterdam was a prosperous one. Wildlife was plentiful; springs provided pure drinking water; wheat, rye, and barley grew in abundance. The population was a blend of French, Dutch, and English; many of these colonists had left their native lands seeking religious freedom, just as Deborah had. The town was set on a marsh and salt meadow, and the settlers claimed the climate to be "the best in the whole world."

Deborah and her followers were greeted warmly by Governor William Kieft, but they soon discovered the governor claimed great powers for himself and expected settlers to join the Dutch Reform Church. Kieft was unable to maintain cordial relations with the local Indian tribes, which led to frequent raids on the settlement.

Other English settlers in New Amsterdam were searching for a new community. Nicholas Stillwell had arrived from England in 1638. Edward and William Browne had also left Massachusetts when threatened with prosecution by John Endecott. Deborah's son, Sir Henry, had recently arrived from England. The group visited Governor Kieft and petitioned to be allowed to start their own community, where they could make their own rules.

Among the reasons the settlers in New Amsterdam were beginning to challenge Kieft's authority was his cruel treatment of the Indians. He believed Deborah and her followers might act as a buffer to the Indians, so he granted them a patent for a tract of land on the southwest corner of Long Island. The settlement would be called Gravesend.

From the beginning Gravesend was different. It did not evolve haphazardly as most new settlements did. It was a planned community, spread over a sixteen-square-acre tract. The tract was divided into four squares of four acres each with two roads bisecting it—one north-south and one east-west. There were ten house lots to each square, providing forty house lots in all. Outside the four quadrants a series of one-hundred-acre farms, or "boweries," radiated like spokes from a wheel. In the center of the four squares was a wide, public plain designed for the use of all the inhabitants for the grazing of cattle. Later it would provide space for a school, a town hall, and a cemetery. The entire town was surrounded by a palisade fence designed to offer protection against attack from wild animals and marauding Indian tribes.

Need for the palisade was proven even before it was finished. An attack by Indians forced the new settlers to flee to the protection of the fort at New Amsterdam. There they lived for two years until Governor Kieft signed a peace treaty with the local tribes in August 1645. On December 19, 1645, Kieft awarded Deborah and her followers a final patent for the community. The document was written in English, although at that time Dutch was the language used on most official documents. The patentees were Lady Deborah Moody, her son Henry, Ensign George Baxter, and Sergeant James Hubbard, and "their heirs and successors." It is believed to have been the first patent ever granted in the New World with a woman's name heading the list of patentees.

Almost 150 years before the American Bill of Rights, the Gravesend settlers were granted a patent guaranteeing them "free liberty of conscience, without molestation." Although they were subject to some jurisdiction by Kieft and were not permitted to build a church, they would be allowed to govern themselves and, most important to them, would be allowed to worship God freely in their own homes without fear of reprisal from anyone. Such a degree of religious freedom was unheard of in the New World. For it to have been obtained in the name of a woman was truly unbelievable.

The town grew in size; by 1646 twenty-six settlers had been granted plots of land, a number that would eventually grow to forty. Deborah was allocated lots nine and ten with "the loving agreement of the whole town," the only settler to be granted two lots. The settlers of Gravesend would not imitate the Puritans in Salem who persecuted newcomers, but some rules were needed to govern the community. Town meetings were held; all settlers were required to attend. Homesteaders were required to build a "habit-able house" on their property or the land would revert back to the community. They were also required to help maintain the wall that surrounded and protected the settlement. Every owner of a house was required to have a ladder twenty feet tall and was provided

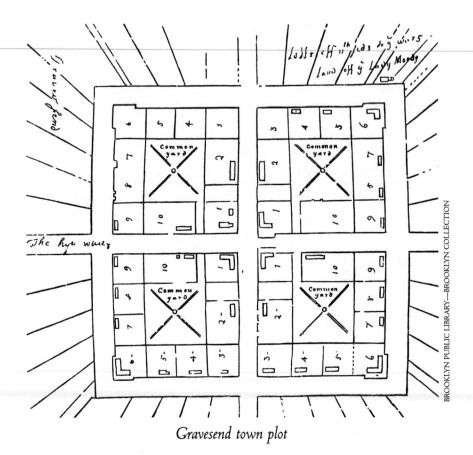

Gravesend town plot

with a gun, a pound of powder, and two pounds of lead. It was also agreed at town meetings that

> whoever should transgress in word or deed in defaming, scandalizing, slandering, or falsely accusing any to the breach of the peace and the reproach of the place, should suffer such . . . punishment according to his demerit, as should be thought meet by the magistrates, either by fine, imprisonment, stocking or standing at a public post.

Deborah participated fully in the election of town magistrates and is believed to be the first woman in the colonies to vote in any election.

Peter Stuyvesant replaced William Kieft as governor in 1647, and although he was an autocratic ruler, relations between Deborah and the new governor were cordial. Stuyvesant believed in paying the Indians for their land, a policy Deborah agreed with. But despite this, the Indian raids continued over the years, occasionally requiring the settlers to turn to New Amsterdam for protection.

In 1652 war broke out across the Atlantic between England and the Netherlands, straining the relations between the English at Gravesend and the Dutch at New Amsterdam. Despite the charter granting them self-rule, Stuyvesant considered it his right to elect Gravesend magistrates. But Peter Stuyvesant respected Deborah's position as town leader. In 1654 he met with her to discuss his dismissal of two Gravesend magistrates, and in an unprecedented display of support for the lady leader, he left the final choice of magistrates in her hands.

He was not pleased in 1657, however, when the first Quakers, persecuted in Massachusetts, came to New Netherlands. Peter Stuyvesant hated Quakers and tormented them vigorously. Deborah respected their religion, partly because of the active role women played in their society. It is not surprising that she welcomed them, invited them to settle in Gravesend, and allowed them to hold meetings in her home. Gravesend ultimately became the center for the Quaker religion on Long Island. It is believed by some historians that Deborah later became a Quaker herself.

Deborah had been born a member of the aristocracy and had enjoyed a life of wealth and privilege in England and to some extent in the New World. But that life was only sustainable if she accepted the religious ideas of others and gave up her own, something unthinkable to her. Deborah never gave up her dream of a peaceful, productive life within which she could worship God freely and live without fear of reprisals for her outspoken and non-conformist beliefs. For a brief fourteen years, she enjoyed those freedoms in Gravesend and ultimately helped established a foothold for them in the New World. She secured a respect for the rights of women by being the first woman patentee and later the first woman to cast a vote in town elections. She showed the colonists the value of study and scholarship; hers was one of the first libraries in the colonies, with over two hundred books of poetry and scriptures that she generously loaned to her neighbors.

She died in 1658 or 1659 at Gravesend. After her death her son became ambassador to Virginia from New Netherlands; he died in 1661. Five years after Deborah's death, the English conquered New Amsterdam, and Gravesend became a part of the borough of Brooklyn in the city of New York.

Now heavily settled, Gravesend is a multiethnic community of homes, restaurants, and apartment buildings. Remnants of the original four-square, sixteen-acre settlement are still faintly visible in the outline of streets. Deborah's house still stands at 27 Gravesend Neck Road. Gravesend Cemetery is the oldest one owned by the city of New York, although Deborah's grave is not listed there.

But more is left of Gravesend than just streets and a cemetery. The freedoms fought for and established by Lady Deborah Moody and her followers in that small, seaside community would influence the history of our nation. The right to freedom of religion would ultimately be adopted throughout the land and would last long after the landing of those first nervous immigrants on her shores. Lady Deborah Moody proved to be not just the Grand Dame of Gravesend, New York, but a Grand Dame of freedom, the first Lady Liberty for the New World.

KATERI TEKAKWITHA

1656–1680

The Lily of the Mohawks

*H*eart pounding, consumed with terror, the young Indian girl plunged headlong into the wild forest. Racing through the undergrowth, she leapt over fallen tree trunks and pushed frantically against the bare branches that sprang back against her scarred face. Stumbling over rocks, she blindly followed her two guides as they tore through the dense underbrush, just steps ahead of the fierce Indian chief who pursued them. At any moment the chief could catch up with them and force the girl to return with him to their Mohawk village home and his pagan way of life.

Suddenly she and her companions burst free of the forest and reached the swollen river. Flinging their canoe into the raging waters, they rowed frantically away, up that river and others, and across lakes. As the miles between Tekakwitha (pronounced *Tek'ak with'a*) and her pursuer lengthened, and she sensed she had eluded him, a great weight lifted from her spirit.

Finally she and the others reached the Christian settlement of Caughnawaga on the banks of the St. Lawrence River, not far from the city of Montreal in Canada. There she would be free to live a chaste and holy life devoted to her religious beliefs. Many would turn to her for help in their spiritual needs. In death she would bridge the gap between the white world and the Native American world as the first Native American to be declared "Blessed" by the Roman Catholic Church, one of the first steps to sainthood.

The forest that Tekakwitha and her companions had raced through was part of a vast, untamed wilderness that sprawled across New York State and was home to the five tribes of the powerful Iroquois Nation: Mohawks, Oneidas, Onondagas, Cayugas, and Senecas. Her journey was the reverse of one her mother, Kahenta, had made many years before. Kahenta was an Algonquin woman who had been baptized as a Christian and who had lived at the Catholic Mission of the Three Rivers, among the French in Quebec. Kahenta had been abducted during a Mohawk raid of the settlement and carried off to become a slave in the Mohawk village of Ossernenon, near the present-day village of Auriesville, New York. Treated harshly by the women elders of the tribe, Kahenta had responded with a Christian spirit of com-passion and tolerance, accepting her duties with quiet dignity and grace.

In time Kahenta's gentle nature caught the attention of the village war chief, Kenhoronkwa, who took the unusual step of marrying her, thus elevating her status from that of a slave to the wife of a great chief. The others in the village grew to respect her. They greeted with joy the birth of the couple's first child, Tekakwitha, in 1656, and her brother soon after. Tekakwitha's name is thought by some scholars to mean "she who puts things in order" and by others to mean "she who cuts the way before her."

Tekakwitha's early years were spent securely within her small family circle. The vast and seemingly endless wilderness that was their home offered a comfortable life for the Iroquois—abundant game for food; fertile soil in which to grow corn, squash, and beans; and rich, deep forests that provided berries, nuts and fruits. As the daughter of a chief, her life was tranquil and protected. Her mother quietly taught her about the Catholic religion through prayers and cheerful stories of the saints that she herself had learned at the Catholic mission. She wished her children to be baptized in the Catholic faith, but knew it was impossible—her husband and the tribe would not allow it.

Although the Iroquois Nation was often at war with hostile neighboring tribes and had sometimes battled with the French, within their own tribe the Mohawks were a moral and spiritual people. They honored the Great Spirit, whom they believed watched the good acts of men and rewarded them. Through other religious ceremonies, they demonstrated their respect and gratitude for the natural world around them. They celebrated a feast to honor the maple trees and the sweet sap they provided. The Festival of the Green Corn lasted four days and demonstrated the tribe's respect for this nourishing and vital staple of their diet. Other religious ceremonies demonstrated their belief that the individual was an important and responsible part of the natural whole. Even at a young age, Tekakwitha developed strong religious convictions that were drawn from both the spiritual beliefs of her tribe and Catholic beliefs of her mother.

Tekakwitha was four years old when a smallpox epidemic swept through the tribe, killing her mother, father, and younger brother. She survived a bout with the disease but was left with a horribly scarred face and severely damaged eyesight. Smallpox had been imported into the Iroquois territory by the white man, and it had decimated other tribes as well because the Indians had no resistance to it.

An orphan, Tekakwitha was adopted by her father's brother, Iowerano, who became chief of the tribe in his brother's place. Iowerano and his wife had no children of their own. By adopting

Tekakwitha they naturally wished to care for their niece, but they also hoped the girl would eventually marry, bringing into the family a warrior who would help to continue the family's line. Tekakwitha's Aunt Anastasia also moved into the family's lodge to care for Tekakwitha. Anastasia had been devoted to Kahenta. Now it was Anastasia's job to continue to instruct Tekakwitha in the Catholic religion and to keep the memory of the child's mother alive.

No matter their rank, all Mohawk children were expected to work alongside their elders for the good of the tribe. Even though she was the adopted daughter of a chief, Tekakwitha took her turn cutting wood for the fires and hoeing and weeding the crops in the fields. Because her eyesight was poor, she preferred to work indoors, pounding corn and preparing animal skins for clothing. She was particularly skilled at using beads and quills to create elaborate designs. She also worked on the wampum belts and decorated clothing worn by other tribal members. But she did not readily join in the games and play with the other children of the tribe, preferring a more isolated life inside the lodge.

Throughout Tekakwitha's life the Iroquois Nation faced continuing hostilities with the French, and in 1666 the French again invaded their land, destroying three Mohawk villages, including Ossernenon. Tekakwitha and her family were forced to move to a neighboring area and build a new village, which they named Gandaouague. Peace terms were finally agreed on in 1667. The Mohawks agreed to allow the French priests, whom they called the "Blackrobes," into their villages to counsel and preach to their people.

The Iroquois were naturally suspicious of the Blackrobes. Other white men had sided with their enemies, had taken their lands, and challenged their religion. But as a sign of his willingness to cooperate peacefully, Chief Iowerano welcomed the Blackrobes into his lodge, offering them a place to stay in the village while they preached and tried to convert the Indians to Catholicism. Tekakwitha was fascinated by the priests' piety and kindness and their exciting tale of the birth of the Christ child. It reminded her of the ways of her mother, who had instructed Tekakwitha in the Christian virtues of humility, modesty, and charity. But she was too young to risk alienating her uncle, who did not approve of the Catholic religion, so she cared for the physical needs of the Blackrobes, bringing them food and drink, never mentioning her growing desire to pursue their religion.

The Iroquois way of life was not a gentle one. Rules of the tribe were strictly imposed. One of those rules was that young women must marry at an early age. Such strictures were designed to safeguard both the strength of the tribe and the well-being of the young women themselves. The young had to marry and produce strong, healthy children to continue the work of the tribe. Marriage offered a young woman the protection of a strong warrior in a hostile world.

Marriage also conferred enhanced status on a woman. Unlike white women of the era, Iroquois women held important and influential positions in the tribe. Women were the undisputed leaders of the villages and longhouses. They voted on whether the tribes would go to war. A mother had even more voice in the tribe and could cast additional votes in the tribal conferences. It was the women who were charged with deciding the fate of captives during wars, and they could be merciless, inflicting horrible tortures.

But in her first open defiance of her tribe's laws and customs, Tekakwitha refused to even consider the subject of marriage. She announced that she wished to remain a virgin for her whole life, a preposterous idea, one far beyond the understanding of her family. Her aunts continually pressured her to accept one of the eligible young men of the tribe as a husband. Following custom, they invited a young warrior into their lodge for a meal. When it came time to serve him his food, they asked Tekakwitha to offer him the bowl, knowing full well that such an offer would mean that she was accepting him as her husband. Tekakwitha rose and left the house abruptly and did not return until the young man had left.

Her aunts were angry. Once a cherished stepdaughter, Tekakwitha now became an outcast, expected to perform the most menial chores, mocked, laughed at, derided by other members of the clan. She was suspected of harboring an aversion to the Mohawk men because of her Algonquin heritage and to the Mohawk and Iroquois way of life because of her mother's religious beliefs. There were rumors her mother had set her against marriage before she died. The entire tribe thought Tekakwitha had gone mad.

Tekakwitha was adamant in her refusal to marry, but she remained docile and compliant in all other ways. When the Jesuit priest Father Jacques de Lamberville again visited her village, she finally told him of her wish to be baptized in the Catholic religion. She also confessed to him the desire to remain a virgin for the rest of her life.

One can only wonder at Father's de Lamberville's reaction to this confession by an eleven-year-old girl. He must have been delighted to have another convert to what he himself believed to be the one true religion. But he must have also been concerned about her welfare. Her open refusal to marry and to follow tribal custom had resulted in ostracism and punishment. Who knew what punishment would be inflicted on her for the adoption of Catholicism by this pagan society? He cautioned her against rashness, advising her to study and pray and to remain respectful of her uncle and her aunts.

Tekakwitha followed his instructions for nine years. During those years she prayed, studied, followed the tenets of the religion as best she could, and moved deeper and deeper into a spirit of religious mysticism. Father de Lamberville continued to instruct her and others in the tribe, including her Aunt Anastasia. In time her uncle and aunts withdrew their objections, even accepting her decision not to marry. Finally on Easter Sunday 1676, Tekakwitha was baptized and formally received into the Catholic faith. She was given the name of Katharine, or Kateri, in honor of Saint Catharine of Siena. She was twenty years old.

Christianity became more established in the tribal communities as the number of converts increased. But even as tribal leaders tolerated these conversions, they still expected their members to continue the Iroquois way of life and to contribute to the well-being of their own people. Tekakwitha's uncle was particularly concerned about converts leaving the tribe and taking away valuable members who were needed to maintain the community's strength and vigor. There were rumors of a settlement in Canada where converts to Catholicism could worship freely and live among Iroquois of their faith. As much as he loved Tekakwitha, he was adamantly against her leaving the tribe.

As a Catholic, Tekakwitha evoked hostility because she would not work on Sundays or on the church's feast days. She began to seek more time alone, moving into the forest to pray and meditate. She withdrew from the activities of the young people of the tribe and avoided tribal celebrations, finding them heathen and cruel. The drunkenness and pagan activities of the tribe sickened her. Her devotion to the Blessed Mother grew, and she carried her rosary with her everywhere.

The community again began to lose patience with her. She was accused of speaking to her uncle in too familiar a fashion, of even perhaps having an immoral relationship with him. Both young and old began to taunt her, to make obscene gestures at her when she passed, and to contemptuously refer to her as "the

Christian." Her religious conversion was making ordinary life within the tribe very difficult for her, and many members of the tribe did not understand such consuming devotion to an alien belief. Father de Lamberville began to fear for her safety and for her mental stability.

One day Tekakwitha's village was visited by the Oneida chief named Okenratariken, also known as Hot Cinders because of his explosive temper and strong beliefs. Hot Cinders was a highly respected chief who had converted to the Catholic faith some time before. His home was now the Mission of the Saulte in Canada, but he often traveled throughout the Iroquois Nation spreading the doctrine of Christianity. Endowed with a natural eloquence, Hot Cinders described his Catholic beliefs in terms the natives could understand and also described the beauties of the Catholic Mission of the Saulte, where Christians worshipped freely in a joyful and prosperous community.

Accompanying him was another resident of the Mission of the Saulte—or Caughnawaga, as the Indians called it—a relative of Tekakwitha's who was married to a girl who had been brought up with Tekakwitha in the same longhouse and who considered herself to be Tekakwitha's sister. This sister was also a Christian and wished to have her husband bring Tekakwitha back with him to the settlement at Sault St. Marie. Tekakwitha's Aunt Anastasia had already gone to live at the mission. Both Tekakwitha and Father de Lamberville believed she belonged with these relatives. But they also knew that Tekakwitha's uncle would never agree to her leaving his home.

It seemed that providence smiled on Tekakwitha the day Hot Cinders and her brother-in-law came to the village. Her uncle was away signing a treaty with the Dutch at Fort Orange. Time was of the essence. They must move quickly to get her away as fast and as far as possible before her uncle returned.

Tekakwitha packed quickly, bidding her aunts farewell. She and the others fled the village, racing through the deep forests in a frantic rush to freedom.

When Chief Iowerano returned to the village and found Tekakwitha missing, he was angry, and he probably felt betrayed by the favorite niece he had cared for after the death of her parents. He took up his gun, loaded it with three bullets, and set off to find her and bring her back. Halfway through the forest he came upon Tekakwitha's brother-in-law, sitting calmly on a log, smoking his pipe. But Iowerano had never met the man before, so he moved on, while Tekakwitha hid behind a tree, holding her breath. When they were certain Iowerano was gone, the three resumed their flight and finally reached the river. Hot Cinders gave Tekakwitha his place in the canoe and moved on to preach at another village. Tekakwitha and the brother-in-law sailed away to freedom. What became of Chief Iowerano remains a mystery. There is no record of him ever returning to his village.

A likely path the fugitives followed was up the Hudson River, on to Lake George, and across Lake Champlain. After three weeks of travel, they reached the settlement of Caughnawaga in the fall of 1677. Tekakwitha carried with her a letter from Father de Lamberville to the resident priests at the settlement, Fathers Cholonec and Chauchetiere. "You will soon know what a treasure we have sent you," he wrote. "Guard it well then!" Kateri Tekakwitha's new life had begun.

Tekakwitha was joyfully reunited with her Aunt Anastasia, moved into her home, and immediately began to study to receive her First Communion. She attended two Masses each day. She carried her rosaries and prayed to the Blessed Mother. Finally on Christmas Day, 1677, she received Holy Communion for the first time. Father Cholonec described her early days at the settlement: "In a few weeks she stood out among all the other women and girls of the mission . . . in a short time a saint among the just and faithful."

But life at the Mission of the Sault was not without problems. Despite their Christian way of life, the Native Americans who lived at the mission kept many of their native practices, including going out on hunting expeditions, during which they left the mission for months at a time. Everyone was expected to take part in these expeditions. Tekakwitha drew the anger of the settlement when she refused to go because it meant long absences from Mass and the Sacraments. Once again it was suggested that she marry, and once again she refused, pledging herself to the life of a virgin and consecrating herself totally to the Blessed Mother. She and another Native American woman considered beginning their own community of nuns, an action that was discouraged by the priests of the settlement.

In the spirit of the Christian martyrs, Tekakwitha began a program of self-punishment that she continued until her death that she considered necessary as atonement for her sins. She walked in the snow without moccasins, slept on a bed of thorns, and fasted for days. She seemed determined to rise to a new level of holiness, using personal mortification as the cornerstone of her spirituality. After all her Native American upbringing prized and admired brave stoicism in the face of pain. Now she had a positive reason for suffering.

She again withdrew from the community, spending long hours in prayer, increasing her personal penance, even wearing an iron waist chain to increase her suffering. The villagers finally sensed that she was a soul apart and sought her counsel and guidance in spiritual matters. Finally the harsh life she inflicted upon herself began to take its toll, and her health began to fail. She was confined to her cabin, where she died on April 17, 1680. She was twenty-four years old.

Reports of Tekakwitha's saintliness spread almost immediately. Those who were present at her death told of a miraculous transformation of her features. The marks from her childhood bout with smallpox disappeared, and her skin lightened and became radiant. The Native Americans at the Sault Mission began almost immediately to call her "The Saint."

Hundreds of people came to her grave at Caughnawaga, Quebec, Canada, to pray. The ill came and asked to be healed. Many cures were reported. Several people told of personal visits by her after her death. Anastasia said Tekakwitha came to see her and was "radiant and lovely, carrying a shining cross." Father Cholonec reported that she visited him and asked him to paint her portrait. When the portrait was finished, it too was reported to be the source of miracles and cures of the lame and the ill. By 1695 there had been hundreds of claims of miraculous cures reported, and reverence for the young woman grew.

An example of such devotion was evidenced in a letter written in 1682 by Father Chauchetiere to a friend in France:

We cease not to say Masses to thank God for the graces that we believe we receive every day through her intercession. Journeys are continually made to her tomb, and the savages following her example have become better Christians than they were. We daily see wonders worked through her intercession.

In 1932 the accounts of her life that had been recorded by Father de Lamberville, Father Chauchetiere, and other missionaries contributed significantly to the documentation necessary for her to be canonized as a saint. In 1942 she was declared by the Roman Catholic Church in Rome to be Venerable, and private devotion to her was allowed. In June 1980 Pope John Paul II declared her to be Blessed, another important step in her journey toward sainthood.

Tekakwitha turned away from the pagan culture of her birth and lived in a world steeped in holiness and piety. Yet she exhibited enormous strength. She successfully challenged her community on several issues that were considered fundamental to the tenets of the group. Although Iroquois women had many rights within their communities, religious freedom and the choice to remain unmarried were not among them. Tekakwitha fought for her right to remain single and to worship as she chose. She endured ostracism, pain, and danger for the freedom to follow her Christian principles. She was the first Native American woman known to make a vow of chastity and to live a life of penitential spirituality. Her unflagging belief that it was the wish of God that she do so carried her from the relative obscurity of the Iroquois Nation to the very portals of sainthood—the first Native American to be so honored.

Today veneration of Kateri Tekakwitha goes on, as the case for her sainthood continues to be heard in Rome. At the shrine at Auriesville, New York, she is honored for her purity of faith and her devotion to God. Her feast day is celebrated on July 14. Over three hundred years after her death, devotion to "The Lily of the Mohawks" is alive and flourishing.

SYBIL LUDINGTON
1761–1839

The Female Paul Revere

$\mathcal{S}$ybil Ludington was cold—far colder than she had been in her sixteen years. The cold set her teeth to chattering and turned her hands to ice. The wet, dark night was only partially to blame. The rest perhaps could be laid to an emotion she was only just beginning to become familiar with: fear—bone deep, icy as a mountain stream, tenacious as the night.

But if fear was her enemy, it was the lesser of those she faced that night, alone on her pony on a dark, rain-swept road. There was a war being fought. Enemy British troops were burning a nearby city. There were outlaws about, preying on British sympathizers and American revolutionaries alike. They would not treat kindly a young girl out alone on a patriot's mission in the middle of the night. There were the dangers of the road itself—unpaved, slick with icy rain, studded with shadowy ditches and pitfalls. No, fear would have to wait its turn. Sybil Ludington could not afford the luxury of indulging it; there was too much else to worry about. She gathered her cloak around her slender shoulders, dug her heels into her pony's flanks, and rode off into her own special place in history.

Sybil Ludington was born on April 5, 1761, the eldest of a family that would eventually include twelve children. Her mother, Abigail, was the daughter of her father Henry's uncle, Elisha, making her parents first cousins. Abigail didn't even have to change her last name when she married.

Henry was a career soldier who fought in the French and Indian War from 1756 to 1769. He swore an oath of loyalty to the king of England and served under William Tryon, captain-general of the Province of New York. Tryon appointed him captain of a Fredericksburgh regiment of militia in Duchess County. But the revolutionary fever that was sweeping through the young colonies caught at Henry's heart. He eventually abandoned his allegiance to the king and joined with the patriots in their fight for freedom. In 1776 a newly formed provincial Congress granted him the title of colonel and assigned him an area of command in Duchess County, New York.

Henry and Abigail lived in the small village of Fredericksburgh, New York, east of the Hudson River, not far from the Connecticut line. There they built and maintained a prosperous farm, sawmill, and gristmill and raised their large family under the constant shadow of war. Abigail was often called on to work the gristmill and tend to the farm and children by herself because the regiment Henry commanded could be summoned to fight at a moment's notice. As well, the community had to maintain a constant guard against marauding bands of outlaws called "Cowboys" and "Skinners" (named for General Courtland Skinner). These groups roamed the area and preyed on everyone indiscriminately. They attacked women, robbed homes and travelers, and stole horses and supplies to sell to the highest bidder. Henry was on constant guard against these outlaws and thwarted their actions whenever he could. Because the outlaws had connections to the British, there was a price of three hundred

English guineas on Henry's head; he was wanted by the British "dead or alive." Fortunately the reward was never collected. Although the family was close-knit and prosperous, such turbulent times made life for all of them very difficult, and they lived under constant threat of violence and death.

The British had heard rumors that the Continental army was storing military supplies in the city of Danbury, Connecticut, and had left only about 150 soldiers on hand to defend these stores. Henry's former commander, General William Tryon, had been ordered to take his 2,000 troops and march to Danbury, destroy those supplies, rout out the patriots, and burn their homes and storehouses.

On April 25, 1777, General Tryon and his troops sailed from New York Harbor. They landed at Compo Beach at the mouth of the Saugatuck River near Fairfield, Connecticut, and began their march north to Danbury. Along the way they were attacked by small regiments of patriots, but although they suffered some casualties, they marched on undeterred. At about three o'clock on April 26, they arrived in Danbury and promptly set the town afire, burning storehouses and barns, destroying arms and supplies, including grain and meat. The soldiers also found abundant stores of rum, and many became hopelessly drunk. Arms linked, they wove their way through the streets, shouting and swearing at the residents. Only the properties of Tories, known British loyalists, were spared the torch, and these were marked with crosses to identify them. There were casualties on both sides.

Throughout the surrounding countryside the patriots began to rally. As the flames from the fires filled the night sky, dispatchers rode frantically throughout the countryside, spreading the word that Danbury was under siege and was sorely in need of defense.

The evening calm of the small village of Fredericksburgh was shattered by the arrival of a lone, exhausted courier. Galloping into

Colonel Ludington's yard at about nine o'clock, he dropped off his horse and pounded furiously on the door of the Ludington family's home. "Danbury's burning!" he shouted as Colonel Ludington opened the door to the exhausted man. They both looked to the east and saw the reddening in the night sky coming from the fires at Danbury. "Tryon's raiding Danbury," he sputtered again, as he fell exhausted to the ground. "We must muster the troops to defend the city."

Because Colonel Ludington had served under William Tryon, he knew him well. Something told him that if William Tryon were allowed to continue his rampage, he would not be satisfied with just torching Danbury and the supplies stored there. He would continue on, burning a swath of destruction through Connecticut and into New York's Hudson Valley. But many of the American militia units had been disbanded to allow the men to go home for the spring planting. How would he notify them that they were now sorely needed? The call had to go out immediately, to be passed from farm to farm and from village to village, through the winding roads of the sleeping countryside. There was not a minute to waste.

Colonel Ludington saw that the courier was too tired to ride farther. The colonel himself could not go. He was needed at home to give the men who gathered orders and help formulate battle plans. There was only one other person he knew of capable of such an enormous task.

"I can go. Let me go, Father." Did Sybil volunteer before she was asked, or did her father ask first? Historical accounts differ. Nonetheless the idea made sense. Sybil was a strong rider with an equally strong young pony named Star. She had accompanied her father many times on his rounds to visit the men in his regiment and knew where they all lived. She was the oldest, the most competent of all the children. And she wanted to go.

Such a ride was terribly dangerous. In addition to the dangers of a rain-swept road and the dark night, Sybil's parents knew of the other dangers—including the Cowboys and Skinners who roamed the forests. To send a young girl off on such a dangerous mission was courting disaster.

But although Sybil was only sixteen, she was certainly no longer a child. The hardships of war had shortened her childhood and had caused her to mature at an earlier age. Colonial children even younger than Sybil were often fully engaged in the war effort with their families, traveling long distances to evade the enemy, billeting troops in their homes, and providing soldiers with food and clothing to take on the road.

The war upset many long-held tenets regarding family and social structure as well, especially those defining the roles of women. A group whose political opinions had seldom held much weight before was suddenly called on to take part in political actions, such as boycotting tea and luxury goods from England. Sybil and her mother had already joined the ranks of colonial women who had taken over the responsibility of family businesses and the defense of their homes and families while the men were away. Given the social structure of the day, it would not be out of the question for Sybil to undertake such a ride. But it was still very dangerous and caused her parents great concern.

In the end practicality and her young resolve won them over. Sybil dressed hastily in a pair of her father's old trousers. Her mother wrapped her in a warm cloak and slipped some food in her pocket for the long journey. Her father offered her a strong stick for banging on the shutters to wake the sleeping soldiers. He cautioned her to take care of herself and her horse. "Keep your eyes and ears open," he warned. "If you hear footsteps or voices, pull off the path and hide until they pass." Sybil listened carefully, mounted her pony, gathered the hempen reins in her hands, and galloped off into the night.

She rode through a cold, driving rain, following the path of a stream, visiting house after house. With her stick she banged on the shutters to wake the soldiers, shouting at them to "muster at Ludington's—the British are burning Danbury." From farm to farm the alarm was spread, and those she alerted in turn alerted others. Despite her resolve to be brave, she must have had to control her fear. She had to listen for the hoofbeats of other horses and watch for the flickers of the campfires that would mark the presence of outlaws and drifters. She must certainly avoid the homes of the British loyalists who would doubtlessly try to detain her. And there was not only herself to worry about. She had to consider her pony, Star. He had to be guided around potholes and over slick, rutted roads. Suppose he tired before the ride was over or, even worse, broke a leg?

Sybil Ludington's ride is often compared with that of Paul Revere, the American silversmith who also fought bravely during the American Revolution. Revere attended the Boston Tea Party and often acted as a courier, carrying messages aiding the patriot cause. On the night of April 18, 1775, two years before Sybil's ride, he rode with two others from Boston to Concord to warn Samuel Adams and John Hancock of the approach of British troops.

But a comparison between the two rides shows that Sybil's was the more daring and certainly the more dangerous. Revere was a grown man who rode with two others and who had other couriers to help him along the way. Sybil was a young girl who rode alone. Revere's ride was shorter than hers, probably about 15 or 20 miles. Hers was about 40. And Paul Revere never actually reached Concord, being detained by British scouts between Lexington and Concord. Only another member of his party was actually able to get through to warn the militia. Sybil completed her ride successfully and returned home in the early morning light to find over four hundred militiamen had mustered as the result of her call.

In 1907 Henry Ludington's grandchildren, Lavinia Elizabeth and Charles Henry Ludington, published Colonel Ludington's memoirs, which included the following passage:

> There is no extravagance in comparing her ride with that of Paul Revere and its midnight message. Nor was her errand less efficient than his. By daybreak, thanks to her daring, nearly the whole regiment was mustered before her father's house in Fredericksburgh, and an hour or two later was on the march for vengeance on the raiders.

At Danbury, Tryon was still having trouble controlling his drunken troops. Hearing news that local militiamen were rallying, he decided to abandon Danbury and return to his ships anchored in Long Island Sound. But before he left, he ordered his troops to continue burning patriots' property. The final tally of burned buildings included nineteen homes and twenty-two storehouses and barns.

The British abandoned Danbury with the city burning at their backs. But they soon discovered that their return march to their ships would not be an easy one. Colonel Ludington's regiment joined with others led by Generals Wooster, Silliman, and the then-patriot Benedict Arnold, and together they encountered the British troops at Ridgefield, Connecticut. Although the British outnumbered them three to one, the Colonial forces bravely engaged them, using techniques that they had perfected in previous battles. They hid behind trees and fences and fired on the enemy, repeatedly harassing and attacking them and forcing them back to their ships in what was called by many a "panic-stricken rout." The Colonials suffered casualties—Benedict Arnold had his horse shot out from under him, and General Wooster received an injury that he would die from a few days later. But at Compo Beach, the British soldiers were driven into their waiting ships in such confusion that many drowned.

Colonel Ludington's memoirs reported that "there were far greater operations in the war than this, but there was scarcely one more expeditious, intrepid and successful." The war was far from over, but Sybil had done her part to help the patriots pave the way to victory. Some historians report that later General Washington visited Sybil in her home to personally thank her for her part in the battle.

In 1783 a peace treaty was signed and the war between Britain and the colonies was over. Sybil's life settled down to more comfortable domesticity. In 1784 she married Edward Ogden, who had served on both land and sea during the war and was later an innkeeper. They had one child, Henry. She was widowed in 1799 and later moved with Henry and his family to Unadilla, New York, where she lived until her death on February 26, 1839. Henry grew up to become a lawyer and serve in the state assembly in 1820. The story of Sybil's remarkable ride was unknown until 1907 when Henry Ludington's grandchildren discovered it while reading his memoirs.

Sybil Ludington epitomized perfectly the bravery, youth, and patriotism of the new nation struggling to emerge from British rule at the end of the eighteenth century. History was slow to recognize her contribution to the American Revolution, but recognition has come. In 1935 the Enoch Crosby Chapter of the Daughters of the American Revolution joined with several other organizations to honor Sybil and her midnight ride by placing a series of historic roadside markers along her route. The trail runs about 40 miles through Putnam and Duchess Counties in New

Statue honoring Sybil Ludington

York State and can be followed by car today. In 1975 the U.S. Postal Service issued a Sybil Ludington stamp to help commemorate the American Bicentennial by honoring young American heroes and heroines. Numerous poems, songs, and articles have been written about her, and children in New York State routinely learn about her famous ride in their American history classes.

In 1961 noted sculptress Anna Hyatt Huntington created a magnificent bronze statue of Sybil, which stands on the shores of sparkling Lake Gleneida, near Carmel, New York. The young girl holds her stick high above her head. Her pony rises in flight beneath her. She is poised to ride for freedom, and through her own modest contribution to that cause, she rides into history, changing her life and that of her country forever.

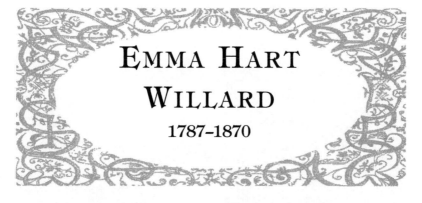

EMMA HART WILLARD
1787–1870

Champion of Education for Women

*T*he young woman sat pensively gazing out the window while the late afternoon sun cast lengthy shadows across the lawn. Across the street of the small New England town where she lived with her husband and family, the Middlebury College campus fairly hummed with activity. The young men hurried to and from their classes in Greek, Latin, mathematics, and geometry, while the chapel bells chimed the hours, calling them to their studies.

The young woman watching them was no stranger to academics—indeed she had been a teacher for much of her adult life. Emma Hart Willard began teaching at the age of seventeen in the village school in Berlin, Connecticut, that she herself had attended. But the subjects she had drilled her students in— reading, ciphering, and simple historical facts—were very different from those the young men of Middlebury College were studying. Most of her students were boys, because there was a general hesitancy on the part of the taxpayers to pay for the education of

Emma Hart Willard

girls. Only in later years had she been permitted to teach girls, and then only during the summer months.

But now she was beginning to discover just how lacking her own education had been, and how lacking were educational opportunities for other women. Her husband's nephew lived with them while he attended Middlebury College, and he cheerfully joined her active household of five children, piling his books on the table for her to read. He discussed his subjects with her and encouraged her to study with him. And the more she read his books, the more she studied and mastered such difficult subjects as geometry and philosophy, the more convinced she became that the level of education available to women would have to change.

As she sat nursing her infant son, watching the young men rush to and from class, she did not imagine herself a revolutionary, though she was about to become one. She simply hungered for the access to higher education that men took for granted. She was frustrated by the prejudice faced by her sex. But the method of attaining that goal was elusive. For the moment she was concerned with getting along with her four stepchildren and running her active household. For the time being revolution would have to wait.

Emma Hart was born February 23, 1787, the sixteenth child of a Revolutionary War captain. Revolution was in her blood. Her ancestors railed against religious strictures in England. They sailed to the New World seeking religious freedom and founded the Connecticut towns of Hartford and Farmington. Her father fought in the American Revolution, leading a company of volunteers who defended the coastal towns of Connecticut against invasion by British forces.

When the Revolutionary War was over, Samuel Hart eagerly returned to farming and to raising his large family. During the war his first wife, Rebecca, had died; his second wife was Lydia Hinsdale, a capable young woman, well educated and cultured and not afraid of hard work. She joined Samuel in raising his seven children and produced ten more, including Emma.

The Harts were a close-knit family who shared affection and the hard work of the farm. The girls of the family helped in the loom room, carding, spinning and weaving the wool from the family's sheep. Both wool and flax were spun and woven into cloth for the family's clothes. But it was not all work—there were corn huskings and quilting bees and large family parties with feasts and merriment.

The end of the war had not quenched Samuel's passion for revolution or for the challenge of new and liberal ideas. When the farm work was finished in the evening, the family gathered around the fire to listen to Father's tales of war, of the bravery of such men as George Washington and the Marquis de Lafayette, and of the thrill of battle and the excitement of founding a new nation. Emma's mother would read to the family from the works of Chaucer and Shakespeare or from Thomas Paine's *Age of Reason*. From these close family experiences, Emma developed a fierce and burning patriotism and a devotion to learning and scholarship.

But during her childhood years, Emma didn't know that young women were not supposed to strain their "weak" brains trying to understand politics or current events. At the end of the eighteenth century, prevailing public opinion held that advanced education for women was not only unnecessary, but it also could be harmful. Taxing the delicate female brain with history and literature might invoke madness—or might even result in witchcraft! Many churches taught the belief that women's brains were created by God to be inferior to men's. To tamper with such design was against the Creator's wishes and would only cause chaos and madness.

Women should learn to read only as much as was needed for a simple study of the scriptures. The remainder of their education should be devoted to music and dancing and to the household skills of cooking and needlework. Female education was tolerated only for the benefits it would bring to husbands and sons. It was never encouraged simply for its own sake—for the fulfillment and enjoyment it might bring to the woman herself.

Emma was more fortunate than most girls; her father was devoted to her and took pleasure in her mental gifts. He encouraged her to study whatever she pleased and often freed her from household chores to read with him or share some of his scholarly pursuits. Samuel recognized the need of the growing young nation for educated citizens, both male and female. Emma attended the local school and later was enrolled in Hartford's Worthington Academy for young girls.

When she was seventeen, Emma was asked to teach at the local school herself. It was an ambitious undertaking for such a young woman; many of her students were not much younger than she and openly challenged her right to discipline them. But she accepted the challenge eagerly, and for several years she alternated teaching in the local school with continuing her own education.

After the relative quiet of the small town of Berlin, Emma found life in Hartford, with its mansions and shops, to be stimulating and exciting. While studying at the academy, she lived with her cousin, Dr. Sylvester Wells, and his wife, Eunice. Dr. Wells was a member of the state constitutional convention and a candidate for Congress. His wife was educated and refined. Their household was alive with liberal political and religious ideas—ideas that made Emma more eager than ever to broaden her educational horizons.

Emma was just twenty years old when she was invited to join the faculty at both Westfield Academy in Westfield, Massachusetts, and at a girl's school in Middlebury, Vermont. She first chose Westfield, but soon left, discouraged by the lack of opportunity for advancement. At Middlebury she was offered full charge of the academy, a post that would provide her with administrative experience but would again illustrate to her how inadequate her own education had been.

She left teaching in 1810 to marry John Willard, a physician and a politician. Twice widowed and twenty-eight years her senior, he came to the marriage with four children. A loyal member of the Republican Party (this was the Jeffersonian party, not the forerunner of today's Republican Party), he held several influential positions in the state of Vermont and owned several farms and a lovely brick home. He was also a believer in advanced education for women, and he encouraged Emma to read and study with his nephew. Their only child, John, was born in 1810.

After three years of marriage, the older John was to appreciate Emma's teaching abilities when a reversal of fortunes put the young family's finances in jeopardy. In the spring of 1814, to ease her family's financial difficulties, Emma returned to teaching and opened a school for girls in the upstairs rooms of the house. Eventually the school welcomed seventy students, forty of them boarders.

The school in Middlebury was to be the proving ground for Emma Hart Willard's then-revolutionary ideas about female education. From the beginning the male establishment offered no support. When she asked that her students be allowed to sit in on college classes at Middlebury College, she was refused. When she asked if she herself might attend the boys' examinations to familiarize herself with the advanced subjects she was planning to teach, she was rebuffed. She considered the male establishment's attitude both shortsighted and perilous, as she wrote to a friend in 1815:

When we consider that the character of the next generation will be formed by the mothers of this, how important does it become that their (the men's) reason should be strengthened to overcome their insignificant vanities and prejudices, otherwise the minds of their sons as well as their daughters will be tinctured by them!

Why didn't the men realize that by educating their daughters they were educating the whole family? Emma firmly believed that marriages would be happier if women were on the same intellectual plane as their husbands. But no one besides her husband and a few close friends agreed with her. She finally realized that if she wanted to develop a program of advanced study for women, she was strictly on her own. Because no one who knew anything about it would help her, she was forced to develop her own curriculum, write her own lesson plans, and train her own teachers.

And so she did just that. She used her own studies to develop lessons in history, geography, mathematics, and science. She wrote texts from the work she had studied in her nephew's books on geometry and philosophy. She used the works of Shakespeare to teach literature and language arts. Unlike the boys' schools, she included art, music, and recreation in the curriculum. She developed her own oral examinations and invited the prominent citizens of Middlebury to witness them. And she showed the public that women could learn advanced subjects without sacrificing their ladylike refinements.

Emma evolved a method for teaching that was unique for the time—and eventually became one of the prime reasons for her success. In a three-step process, she drilled her girls on a subject until she was certain they understood it. She then had them recite it to fix it in their memory. Finally she required that they be able to communicate the essence of the subject back to her. In this way the students mastered the subject themselves and were able to teach it to others.

Even after Emma's reputation as an educator was fully established, it became evident that in order to continue she would need more financial support. Professors were needed to teach subjects such as languages and science that she herself was not schooled in. Books and other library materials were needed. Her dream was to build a school financed with public funds, just as the boys' schools were. She would not call it a college—she was too practical for that. Instead she would call it a seminary, for as she explained "that word . . . will not create a jealousy that we mean to intrude upon the province of men." When plans to locate in Vermont fell through, she and her husband petitioned the state of New York for money for a school to be located in the Hudson River Valley, where easy transport would be available for out-of-state students.

To convince the New York legislature of the benefits of education for women, she wrote her educational plan, entitled *An Address to the Public; Particularly to the Members of the Legislature of New York, Proposing a Plan for Improving Female Education.* Such a daring proposal had never been written by anyone, man or woman, before. Aside from her husband, Emma consulted with no one during its development, fearing it would be regarded as "visionary, almost to insanity." The plan was many pages long, handwritten in the clear, concise penmanship of which she was so proud.

Emma believed her *Plan* would "elevate the whole character of the community." She began by showing the defects in the present practice of education for females, explaining that most of the schools available to the young ladies of the day were temporary institutions, concerned more with teaching their pupils "showy accomplishments, rather than those which are solid and useful." Present schools for young ladies were entirely private and had no laws to regulate them or control what was taught.

Education should seek to bring its subjects to the perfection of their moral, intellectual and physical nature in order that they may be of the greatest possible use to themselves and others; or, to use a different expression, that they may be the means of the greatest possible happiness of which they are capable, both as to what they enjoy and what they communicate.

The *Plan* went on to exhibit a practical design for a female seminary and, finally, show the benefits that society would receive from educating young women. Such an education would especially benefit the children of future generations, Emma wrote, whose well-educated mothers could "watch the formation of their characters with unceasing vigilance, to become their instructors, to devise plans for their improvement, to weed out the vices of their minds, and to implant and foster the virtues."

Through the intercession of a friend the *Plan* was placed in the hands of New York Governor De Witt Clinton, who advocated its immediate adoption by the state legislature. Encouraged by his support, Emma and her husband opened a school in Waterford, New York, in the spring of 1819.

But the legislature ultimately refused to fund the school. Although the *Plan* received praise from across the country from such illustrious names as President Monroe and former presidents Adams and Jefferson, it seemed the majority of the public was still not ready to begin funding the education of their daughters. When a group of concerned citizens in Troy, New York, offered the permanent use of a building and equipment, Emma and her husband moved the school to that city, opening The Troy Female Seminary in September 1821 with ninety students from seven states.

From its beginning The Troy Female Seminary prospered and grew, nourished by Emma's close attention and that of her husband, who also acted as the school physician. The three-step method of teaching that had proved so successful in the Middlebury Academy was again employed, with continued emphasis on full comprehension of the subject studied. Emma did not want her girls to learn in a parrotlike fashion, to be able only to recite before a gathering. She wanted them to develop a full understanding of a subject and to be able to effectively teach it to others.

She expanded the curriculum, adding more courses in history and natural philosophy. Through private funding she was able to hire a professor to teach painting, music, and modern languages. Her school was unique—no other school in the country offered such a comprehensive course of study for young ladies.

Emma never believed in educating women to compete with men. She tried instead to prepare them to be gracious and effective women, whether unmarried or as wives and mothers. Every girl, even those from wealthy homes, was expected to clean her own room and to dress simply and modestly. Expensive laces and jewelry were discouraged. Girls were encouraged to develop good table manners and to pay attention to personal appearance and grooming. Church attendance was compulsory, but the girls' families selected the church their daughters attended. Bible study was part of the curriculum, but Emma was careful to keep the school nonsectarian. Tuition varied according to the courses studied, but room and board together cost about two hundred dollars a year.

Emma deeply cared for the girls, considering them her surrogate "daughters." Many of them had made long and arduous journeys by stagecoach or canal boat to study at the seminary. Those students lived at the school for several years because the return journey to their homes was too long to make often. Emma watched over "her" girls as their mothers would, and they in turn loved and respected her.

She also offered schooling to girls who could not pay the tuition, arranging for them to pay her back from their salaries when they became teachers, thus providing some of the first scholarships in the education field. The Troy Female Seminary was one of the first to train teachers, a selling point that Emma continually used when attempting to secure public funding for the school. She pointed out the growing need for teachers, especially in the developing West, and argued that her female teachers were better educated and could be paid less than men, a claim, though true, that she was later to regret. The reputation of her school was so secure that a certificate from The Troy Female Seminary signed by Emma Hart Willard was the best credential any new teacher could have. Before the first normal school opened in the United States to educate teachers in the late 1830s, Emma had sent over two hundred teachers out across the land.

Emma continued to write texts to support her courses, and other schools began to use them. In 1822 she collaborated with writer and geography expert William Channing Woodbridge to publish *A System of Universal Geography on the Principles of Comparison and Classification.* She would go on to write and collaborate on many other textbooks, including *Ancient Atlas* (to accompany the *Universal Geography*), *Atlas to Accompany a System of the Universal History,* and *Geography for Beginners,* which was designed as an "instructor's assistant." She also wrote and published poetry, including her famous poem, "Rocked in the Cradle of the Deep." Royalties from these books would provide her with a comfortable income for the rest of her life.

In 1825 Emma's husband died. Ironically, because the laws of the early nineteenth century prohibited married women from owning any property in their own name, the school and its property as well as income derived from her books had all been in his name. With his death these reverted to Emma, who added his management duties to her own teaching and writing work. In 1838 she married Christopher C. Yates, a New York physician, but divorced him the following year.

Emma had never been a strong proponent of women's rights, believing that it was more important for women to be educated than to be independent politically. She feared the strident tone of many feminists, including Elizabeth Cady Stanton, a student at The Troy Female Seminary in 1836 and a strong advocate of a woman's right to vote. Emma worried that such stridency would ultimately work against women by discouraging men from supporting the cause of female education.

But as time went on and public funding for women's education was not forthcoming, she began to appreciate the goals of the women's movement, especially in regard to equal pay for equal work. She always felt strongly that women should be financially independent and paid a wage that would enable them to support themselves. Although she was never considered a feminist, her unflagging support for women's education and independence came very close to the ideals of the new women's rights movement.

Times were changing at last. In 1837 Mary Lyon opened Mount Holyoke Female Seminary at South Hadley, Connecticut. Her school, unlike The Troy Female Seminary, had entrance requirements and a regular three-year course. In 1833 Oberlin Collegiate Institute in Oberlin, Ohio, admitted both men and women, black and white, to an advanced course of study. Other colleges began to welcome female students. The number of proponents of the once radical concept of funding the education of girls as well as boys continued to grow until finally equal education for both boys and girls became the law of the land.

Emma Hart Willard died on August 15, 1870. In 1895 The Troy Female Seminary was renamed the Emma Willard School in her honor. In 1910, endowed by a gift from an alumna, the school moved to a new location in Troy, New York. There it still operates today, not just as a college preparatory school for girls, but as a living testament to a remarkable woman whose belief in the unlimited intellectual capabilities of women would not be denied.

AMELIA JENKS BLOOMER

1818–1894

The Well-Dressed Suffragist

A Bloomer costume made its appearance in Sixth Avenue day before yesterday. A crowd of "Conservatives" manifested their hostility to this progressive movement by derision. "New ideas" are compelled to wage fierce battle in this world before they obtain recognition and favor. Two Bloomers appeared in Broadway and two in Washington Square yesterday.

New York Times, September 18, 1851

Amelia Bloomer read such articles in the press with amusement. Such a fuss over a problem that virtually every woman, young or old, faced every day of her life—what to wear. She sat at her desk in the editorial office of *The Lily* and opened letter after letter from women eagerly extolling the virtues of the daring new "Bloomer" outfit and clamoring for information and patterns so they could make the new style of clothing for themselves. The hundreds of letters proved to Amelia how "ready and anxious women were to throw off the burden of long heavy skirts."

Amelia Bloomer wearing the "Bloomer costume"

Amelia had herself thrown off that burden long ago in favor of the outfit that bore her name: trousers gathered at the ankle and worn under a calf-length skirt, with no stays or corsets underneath. She wore the outfit everywhere—out on the streets of her hometown of Seneca Falls, New York; to meetings and gatherings; and to work as the editor of her newspaper, *The Lily*. She found it comfortable, practical, and beautiful. What was all the fuss about?

But the fuss was not, of course, about the clothes themselves. The fuss was over the fact that under the shorter skirt were trousers, traditional male attire and an established symbol of male dominance. Some people said that by wearing trousers women were trying to usurp the male role and with it the privileges and freedoms typically claimed by husbands, fathers, and sons. Would men thus be relegated to secondary roles, expected to take care of the children, cook, and clean the house? How outlandish! How unthinkable! How frightening!

In 1851 the average woman wore long, dark skirts that reached the ground. Underneath were at least four, sometimes six, petticoats, cotton or flannel, depending on the season. These petticoats might be heavily starched and lined and corded with horsehair. Often the bottoms were corded with a stiff, horsehair plait offering a hoop effect that made the underskirts stand out, but also made it difficult to sit and move. Under the petticoats were worn lace-trimmed drawers, a lace camisole, and a corset, usually made of whalebone. The corsets were laced as tight as possible in order to produce the appearance of a small, slim waist. At the same time the arms were often held in a position that made it impossible to lift them. Such attire produced a graceful, lovely vision that was impractical, unhealthy, and downright dangerous to a woman's internal organs.

Not only were the clothes restrictive, they were heavy. The typical woman's daily outfit weighed an average of fifteen pounds and hampered any freedom of movement. Women found it difficult to run, to bend, to stoop, to carry children and parcels— all movements that typically were required of them. They were tired of dragging heavy skirts through the mud, tired of fighting the dirt that the skirts dragged into their homes. Clothing reform was sorely needed, and Amelia Bloomer was ready to champion such reform—beginning with her own closet.

She was uniquely qualified for the job. She was believed to be the first woman to write and edit her own newspaper, *The Lily*, which claimed on its masthead to be "devoted to the interests of women." She counted among her closest friends Elizabeth Cady Stanton, one of the inimitable founders of the women's rights movement, and she would later introduce Elizabeth Cady Stanton to Susan B. Anthony. For years she had championed the cause of temperance, refusing even to take a celebratory drink of wine on her wedding day. And she believed firmly in the rights of women to control their own destinies. If anyone could succeed in changing a firmly entrenched societal tradition, it would most certainly be Amelia Jenks Bloomer.

Amelia was born May 27, 1818, in the town of Homer in Cortland County, New York. Her father, Ananias Jenks, was a clothier by trade. Her mother, Lucy Webb, was a devout Christian who believed advanced education was wasted on young women. As the youngest of six children, Amelia passed a pleasant and uneventful childhood, studying at home with her mother and attending the local school only intermittently. Despite the paucity of her education, at the age of seventeen, she was employed as a teacher and later worked as a governess. In 1840, at the age of twenty-two, she married a young Quaker, Dexter C. Bloomer, and the newlyweds took up residence in the small town of Seneca Falls, New York.

It is doubtful that Amelia could have ever achieved the success she later enjoyed without the unflagging encouragement and support of her husband, Dexter. Dexter believed, as Amelia did, in the equality of women, not even protesting when she struck the word *obey* from their marriage ceremony. He was openly pleased when she spoke her mind, and he encouraged her active participation in the temperance movement, a movement that fought long and hard against the evils of drinking alcohol. As a Quaker, Dexter was used to outspoken women; the Quakers were one of the first denominations to espouse equality for both men and women and the right of women to speak in public. As an editor and part owner of a newspaper, the *Seneca Falls Courier*, Dexter encouraged Amelia to write articles for his paper and the newspaper of the local temperance society, *The Water Bucket*.

The evils of alcohol were evident in the mid-nineteenth century. Its use was widespread: Per capita consumption in 1840 was approximately three times what it would be in 1940. Not only was cheap rum available from the West Indies, but many farmers manufactured their own whiskey, and many working people received a supply of liquor as part of their regular wages. Although some women drank alcohol, most imbibers were men, and the problems associated with high liquor consumption impacted heavily on their families. Drunkenness often resulted in physical abuse of wives and children, as well as extreme poverty resulting from lost wages. Abused children were thought to grow up to be abusers themselves and to account for a large percentage of the "criminal class." This was the "sad lot of the drunkard and his wretched family."

The fight for temperance was a political one and offered one of the first platforms where political activism by women was accepted and encouraged. Women felt comfortable in the movement. By opening meetings with prayers and hymns, the movement cloaked itself with the comfortable legitimacy of religion in a basically Christian culture. Temperance sought to change the behavior of society by encouraging higher levels of self-control and elevated moral values, issues traditionally believed to be women's concerns. Association with such a legitimate and quasireligious political cause offered women a smooth transition from domestic life to a public arena, from a discussion of changing moral values to promoting women's rights.

Such political realities might not have been evident at first to Amelia Bloomer. She joined the fight against alcohol abuse because of personal religious principles. But she was also wise enough to realize that women could only be politically effective when they achieved a "more potent voice both in the making and enforcement of the laws designed to overthrow that great evil." Did not that evil have a direct impact on women's lives? So it only seemed reasonable to her that the fight against the evil of alcohol depended on and was an integral part of the fight for equal rights for women.

Despite holding these beliefs, Amelia was slow to support the women's rights movement. When Elizabeth Cady Stanton moved to Seneca Falls in 1847 and called the Women's Rights Convention there in 1848, Amelia was nothing more than an interested bystander. Although she attended the convention, she did not sign the Declaration of Sentiments demanding equal rights because she and Dexter believed that the push for voting rights for women was too extreme. But she did admire Elizabeth Cady Stanton's sincerity and courage.

For Amelia temperance was the logical place to start in the quest for equal rights. But she and other women activists were frustrated by the male dominance of the temperance movement. They wanted a voice of their own, one that would influence and be influenced by women's experiences and ideas.

In her journal she recorded:

> Up to about 1848–9 women had almost no part in all this temperance work. They could attend meetings and listen to the eloquence and arguments of men, they could pay their money toward the support of temperance lecturers but such a thing as having to say or do further than this was not thought of.

So *these women* decided to start their own newspaper, *The Lily*, with Amelia as editor and chief writer. In the first issue she wrote, "It is *woman* that speaks through *The Lily*. It is upon an important subject, too, that she comes before the public to be heard. Intemperance is the great foe of her peace and happiness . . . surely she has the right to wield the pen for its suppression."

The Lily had originally been devoted to articles on the evils of alcohol. But in 1850 Amelia was outraged to learn that the legislature in the state of Tennessee decided against granting women property rights because "women have no souls." She wrote sarcastically in *The Lily*: "Women no souls! Then of course we are not accountable beings, and if not accountable to our Maker then surely not to man. Man represents us, legislates for us and now holds himself accountable for us. How kind in him, and what a weight is lifted from us!"

She decided at once the tenor of *The Lily* must change and must focus more on women working toward equal rights, including suffrage. "We see and hear so much that is calculated to keep our sex down and impress us with a conviction of our inferiority and helplessness that we feel compelled to act on the defensive and stand for what we consider our just rights."

In the spring of 1849, Amelia's husband was appointed postmaster of Seneca Falls, and he asked Amelia to assume the duties of deputy postmaster, a unique opportunity for a woman. She was working in the post office one day when her friend Elizabeth Cady Stanton came to call with her cousin Elizabeth Smith Miller. Amelia was always happy to see her friend, but this day she was also fascinated by what the two women were wearing—an innovative and daring costume consisting of long pantaloons gathered softly at the ankle, modestly covered with a calf-length skirt.

Elizabeth Smith Miller was the daughter of Gerrit Smith, an activist in antislavery and temperance societies and a good friend of Frederick Douglass, the noted abolitionist. Gerrit Smith ran for president of the United States several times. He openly supported not only equal rights for women, but their right to dress as they pleased, and this included his daughter's innovative and daring new style of dress. Elizabeth Miller had been wearing the costume for some time. She found it very comfortable, especially when working in her garden. She had shown it to her cousin Elizabeth Cady Stanton, who immediately made one for herself.

Amelia was enthralled by the new costume, and a few days later she too was dressed in it. The women found the costume to be comfortable and practical—ideal for an active life. As a mother of small children, Elizabeth Cady Stanton especially like the outfit and announced it made her feel like "a captive set free from his ball and chain, always ready to climb a mountain, jump over a fence, or work in the garden." Amelia promptly wrote about the new costume in *The Lily* because she thought her readers would be interested in a change to more comfortable clothes. And that is when the furor broke loose.

Amelia wrote in her memoirs:

> At the outset I had no idea of fully adopting the style:
> no thought of setting a fashion; no thought that my
> action would create an excitement throughout the civ-
> ilized world and give to the style my name and the
> credit due Mrs. Miller. This was all the work of the
> press. I stood amazed . . . finally someone—I don't
> know to whom I am indebted for the honor—wrote the
> "Bloomer costume" and the name has continued to
> cling, in spite of my repeatedly disclaiming all right
> to it and giving Mrs. Miller's name as that of the first
> to wear such dress in public.

Letters poured into *The Lily* asking about the dress, requesting
patterns so the women could make it for themselves. Circulation
of the paper rose from 500 to 4,000 copies a month. Newspapers
from New York to London picked up the story, sometimes
ridiculing the new fashion, sometimes simply spotlighting it as a
new trend. The short dress was officially called "the Bloomer
Costume," despite Amelia's strong protestations that it had been
worn for the first time by Elizabeth Smith Miller and should be
named after her. Amelia had found the fulcrum upon which to
balance her work in temperance and her growing interest in
women's rights. And it all centered about a pair of men's trousers!

Amelia belonged to the Daughters of Temperance and began
to travel a lecture circuit. She wore the new style of dress
everywhere, "at church, on the lecture platform and at fashionable
parties." She found it most comfortable and practical. The
attention it attracted was also welcome, especially when she found
she could focus that attention on the subjects she cared deeply
about. "If the dress drew the crowds that came to hear me," she

explained, "it was well. They heard the message I brought them and it has borne abundant fruit."

Through the Daughters of Temperance, Amelia met Susan B. Anthony, a young Quaker schoolteacher who had just recently become interested in the women's rights movement. In May 1851 Susan was visiting with Amelia. The two friends planned to attend an antislavery meeting that was being organized in Seneca Falls and listen to the lecture of abolitionist William Lloyd Garrison. Amelia and Susan were walking home from the meeting when they chanced to meet Elizabeth Cady Stanton on a street corner. Amelia was delighted to see Elizabeth and introduced her two friends to each other. They liked each other immediately. Later Elizabeth would write about Susan, "There she stood with her good honest face and her genial smile. I liked her thoroughly." Little did Amelia know that she was bringing together two women who would forge an enduring friendship that lasted over fifty years. They would work together tirelessly for the cause of equal rights for women, and they would change the world forever.

By 1853 Amelia was fully committed to the women's rights movement herself. She toured New York State lecturing with other feminists, and she attended an international temperance conclave in New York City. *The Lily* continued to flourish and published the works of other women writers, including Elizabeth Cady Stanton. Amelia saw no conflict with her ideas on temperance and equal rights. Although she was sometimes criticized in the press, she did not hesitate to rebut this criticism:

> Some of the papers accuse me of mixing Women's Rights with our Temperance, as though it was possible for woman to speak on Temperance and Intemperance without also speaking of Woman's Rights and Wrongs in connection therewith. That woman has rights, we

think that none will deny; that she has been cruelly wronged by the law-sanctioned liquor traffic must be admitted by all. Then why should we not talk of woman's rights and temperance together? Ah, how steadily do they who are guilty shrink from reproof! How ready they are to avoid answering our arguments by turning their attention to our personal appearance and raising a bugbear about Woman's Rights and Woman's Wrongs.

In December 1853 the Bloomers left their much-loved home in Seneca Falls and moved to Mount Vernon, Ohio, where Dexter Bloomer had purchased a part interest in a newspaper, the *Western Home Visitor*. Amelia was sorry to leave her life and friends in Seneca Falls. She wrote in *The Lily* that she hoped her subscribers would not desert them, assuring them that "*The Lily* will continue to be published and its character will be in no wise changed. . . . We bid farewell with an aching heart."

But the move west did not impede Amelia's career as an advocate for her three major causes. She continued traveling and lecturing throughout Ohio and Indiana, carrying her message of reform to these midwestern states. *The Lily* was printed on a new type of steam press. Amelia broke new ground in the publishing field by hiring a woman as typesetter, a Mrs. C. W. Lundy. When the male typesetters from the *Western Home Visitor* refused to work with Mrs. Lundy, Amelia and her husband dismissed them all and hired three other women typesetters. In time three men were also rehired. Thus Amelia and her husband presided over one of the first business offices to hire both men and women to do the same job and to work together.

Amelia and her friends continued to wear the Bloomer costume despite constant ridicule and criticism. They often endured the jeers of crowds and the disapproval of family and friends. Elizabeth Cady Stanton's family disapproved of the outfit so strongly that both her father and her son repeatedly begged her not to wear it. There was constant condemnation in the press and continued pressure on the women to revert to the traditional long skirts.

In 1855 Amelia's life changed yet again when she and Dexter moved to Council Bluffs, Iowa. Both of them had long espoused the idea of western expansion and believed firmly that the western part of the country was not only physically beautiful, but was a land of unparalleled economic opportunity. But Council Bluffs was 300 miles beyond the railroad and had no facilities for publishing or mailing a newspaper with the large circulation of *The Lily*. Amelia was forced to part with the newspaper. She sold it to Mrs. Mary A. Birdsall of Richmond, Indiana.

But she entered into her new life in Iowa with enthusiasm, and once she and Dexter were settled, she again began traveling and lecturing. On January 8, 1856, she appeared before the House of Representatives of the Nebraska legislature to plead the cause of women's suffrage. She spoke at an Omaha Library Association meeting on the need to educate women and traveled to Des Moines to argue the case for women's suffrage before the legislature there. Her home was a welcome spot for traveling suffragists, and she was always delighted to offer hospitality to new settlers coming to join them in settling the West.

After moving to Council Bluffs, Amelia had continued to wear the Bloomer outfit, still finding it comfortable and practical. But finally, after wearing the costume almost continually for eight years, Amelia and her friends decided to give it up. It had done its job too well—much of the attention the women sought for the women's rights movement was being deflected by the Bloomer costume, and they reluctantly agreed to stop wearing it.

In 1865 Amelia and Dexter adopted a brother and sister whose parents had died during the Civil War. The Bloomers had never had any children of their own, and now Amelia began to enjoy a more traditional family life, raising her children and becoming an avid gardener. But she continued to write and lecture for equal rights and suffrage. In 1867 she returned to New York to attend the first meeting of the Woman Suffrage Association and was elected one of its vice presidents. In 1870 she was elected president of the Woman Suffrage Society of Iowa.

Amelia Bloomer died on December 31, 1894, but her ideas decidedly live on. In 1874 Frances Willard founded the Women's Christian Temperance Movement and continued to fight against the evils of alcohol abuse. The organization followed Amelia's lead by advocating temperance and equal rights for women, believing as she did that the benefits of both were interdependent. Its efforts culminated in the passage in 1920 of the Eighteenth Amendment to the Constitution of the United States, which prohibited "the manufacture, sale or transportation of intoxicating liquors within the United States . . . for beverage purposes." The amendment was later repealed by the Twenty-First Amendment.

The Bloomer outfit fell from favor for many years after Amelia and her friends stopped wearing it, but it saw a resurgence in popularity in the 1890s when bicycling and other active sports became popular with women. Its benefits had not changed over the years: It was still healthier, more comfortable, and more practical for an active life than long, heavy skirts and corsets could ever be, "a strike for health and freedom" that has prevailed to this day.

The year 1920 also finally saw the passage of the Twentieth Amendment to the Constitution, which stated "the right of citizens of the United States to vote shall not be denied or abridged by the United States or by any State on account of sex." Neither Amelia nor her friends Susan B. Anthony and Elizabeth

Cady Stanton lived to see this victory, but it never could have come about without their unceasing labor.

It is unfortunate that Amelia Bloomer's name will forever be linked primarily to the pantaloons that she favored because her life involved so much more. She believed firmly that a woman's greatest power lay in her strength of character and intelligence, and that those strengths could overcome the limitations that society imposed on her. Only when a woman could dress as she chose, own property in her own name, earn her own income, support her children, and let her feelings be known at the ballot box could she fulfill her potential and participate more fully in the life around her. In her journal she wrote:

> Women had a part to play in life that St. Paul never dreamed of, and he who lives in the next generation will see greater changes than the past has produced. . . . The world moves and woman must move with it. She inherits the same blood, the same spirit of liberty that descends to her brother and for which her fathers bled and died. To fight against this progression is like fighting against the emancipation of slaves. As the chains of the latter were broken and the oppressed set free—in spite of opposition and Bible argument—so will the All-Father in His own good time and way bring about the emancipation of woman and make her equal with man in power and dominion.

HARRIET TUBMAN
1820 OR 1821–1913

The Moses of Her People

The slave crouched, shivering in the tall, damp grass that edged the river, waiting for darkness to cloak her flight. She had run once before, with three of her brothers, but that time the men had been gripped with fear and had dragged her back home with them. This time she would not turn back. She had come too far. She knew she could no longer return to the plantation to bear the shackles of slavery without revolt.

When darkness finally descended, she continued her journey, winding through the dangerous countryside of eastern Maryland, where runaway slaves had few friends. Reward for their capture was generous, and if men could not find them, their dogs most certainly could. At least she was experienced with the out-of-doors. She knew she must follow the Big Choptank River north. She knew she must make the North Star her guide. If she lost her way, she could always check the trees; she knew moss grew thicker on the north side of the trunk. And she had friends along the way—black and white—who would help her.

A white Quaker woman sheltered her the first night. The next day the woman's husband carried her in a wagon to another friendly house. Step by step, mile by mile, friend by friend, she made her perilous way north. And when she finally stood on the free soil of Pennsylvania, her joy knew no bounds. "When I found I had crossed that line I looked at my hands to see if I was the same person. There was such a glory over everything; the sun came like God through the trees and over the fields, and I felt like I was in heaven."

Harriet Tubman had made her way to freedom in the North, but she would not stay there long. Homesick for her family and horrified to think of them still shackled by slavery, she would risk her life to return south nineteen times to bring others to freedom, including most of her own family.

Harriet Tubman was born a slave around 1820 on a plantation east of the Chesapeake Bay, near the small town of Bucktown in Maryland. She was one of the eleven children of Benjamin Ross and Harriet Green. Her father was a free man, but the rest of the family—mother, brothers, and sisters—were owned by Edward Brodess, who owned so many slaves that he found it profitable to hire them out to others. In her early years Harriet was called Araminta, later shortened to Minty. She took her mother's name, Harriet, when she was grown.

From her earliest years the yoke of slavery hung heavily on Harriet, and she was never content beneath it. Even as a very young child of five or six, she was expected to perform hard labor, cleaning the house and caring for young children. When she displeased her mistress, she was whipped, usually for transgressions that were unavoidable because she was expected to perform labor far too strenuous for a small child. Once she was beaten for stealing a lump of sugar and afterward ran away to spend six days in a pigpen, competing for food with the baby pigs. When she returned, she was beaten again.

The constant physical abuse took its toll. Periodically she would become ill, and the overseer would bring her home to recuperate under her mother's care. But once she was well, she would again be put out to labor, and the beatings and deprivation would begin anew. "I grew up like a neglected weed," she once said, "ignorant of liberty, having no experience of it." Not surprisingly, she also grew up to be rebellious and to battle continually against the tyranny of slavery, even before she was old enough to understand it.

When she was about twelve years old, she convinced her master to allow her to labor out-of-doors instead of in the house. Hired out to a neighboring farmer, she chopped wood, hauled water, tilled his fields, and harvested his crops. She developed strong muscles and physical endurance, and it was said she could hold her own with the strongest of the men. Harriet felt free in the out-of-doors and learned to appreciate the natural treasures of wildflowers, grass, and open sky. She learned the physical locations of the neighboring farms and towns and the geography of the night sky.

Working in the fields also offered her another freedom—that of the music that the slaves used to communicate. The fields rang with songs, many of them brimming with hidden messages of freedom and means of escape. One of the most popular was "Go Down Moses," which had a message so clear that many masters and overseers forbade the slaves to sing it:

When Israel was in Egypt land,
Let my people go.
Oppressed so hard they could not stand.
Let my people go.

Harriet Tubman

Chorus:
Oh, go down Moses
Away down to Egypt's land.
And tell King Pharaoh
To let my people go!

Harriet sang with the other slaves and often made up songs of her own. The whispered messages of the fields spoke of rebellion and dreams of a life of freedom in the North, even as far north as Canada. The time was ripe in the South for such rebellion. In 1831 Nat Turner led a slave revolt in Virginia in which many white people were killed—and many slaves in retaliation. Tensions between slaves and masters grew, with fear on both sides. The slave owners feared similar uprisings, while the slaves feared brutal retaliation. Their songs were filled with even more tales of ships and trains and all manner of escape. Harriet's resentment and daring grew.

One day she left her work in the field and followed a young slave named Jim to a store in a nearby village. The plantation overseer followed them both into the store, and as Jim sought to escape, the overseer called to Harriet for help in stopping Jim's flight. Harriet refused, blocking the overseer's path and enraging him so much that he picked up a two-pound weight from the counter and hurled it, missing Jim and hitting Harriet squarely in the head.

Harriet's injuries were grave. No one thought she would live. Although she eventually recovered, she was left with an identifying dent in her head. She was also left with a lifelong crippling brain injury that caused her to fall asleep suddenly and without warning. Her value as a slave was diminished. Paralyzed by pain, she turned to prayer for comfort.

"Oh Lord, convert the Master," she prayed. "Change the man's heart. If you ain't going to change the man's heart, kill him Lord and take him out of the way so he won't do more mischief." Harriet eventually recovered and returned to work, but she was prone to the sleeping sickness for the rest of her life.

Around 1845, when she was about twenty-five years old, Harriet married John Tubman, a free black, and began in earnest to dream of freedom for herself. She saw herself flying over the countryside like a bird, up to the line that divided slave land from free. Sometimes she heard voices urging her to flee, "Come, arise, flee for your life," they would call to her. But John Tubman had little patience with his wife's dreams of freedom and offered her little comfort.

In 1849 Harriet's earlier wish was granted when her master died. But despite a clause in Brodess's will stipulating that none of his slaves were to be sold out of state, the slaves were fearful of just such a fate. Harriet's father was a free man, and her mother too old to be sold, but there were rumors that she and her brothers were to be sold farther south to work on the chain gangs of the rice and cotton plantations in Mississippi, Louisiana, or Alabama. Work on such plantations was backbreaking and living conditions brutal. Years before Harriet had watched helplessly while two of her sisters were torn from the arms of their children and "sold south." She was terrified of that same fate befalling what was left of her family. She saw her family as a crop being used up and depleted by slavery until nothing would be left. She decided she had no choice but to flee.

Even years later Harriet would not give the exact details of her escape for fear of jeopardizing the safety of those who had helped her and those who would be helped in the future. She was also afraid that if her parents knew, they would be punished for not reporting her flight. But historians do know that she left first with three of her brothers, all of whom became frightened and turned back. Two days later she left again, following the edges of the Greenbriar Swamp, then following the Choptank River, always keeping the North Star in front of her and to the left. She traveled at night, keeping to the swamplands, seeking the help of sympathetic friends. Members of the Quaker religion provided food and lodging. And Harriet's faith in God helped her as well, leading her as she crossed from Maryland to Delaware and finally on to freedom in Pennsylvania.

But after experiencing the initial joy of freedom, Harriet was suddenly overcome with a fierce loneliness. In *Scenes from the Life of Harriet Tubman*, she told her biographer, Sarah Bradford:

> I had crossed the line. I was free . . . but there was no one to welcome me to the land of freedom. My home was down in Maryland because my father, my mother, my brothers, my sisters and friends were there. But I was free, and they should be free. I would make a home in the North and bring them there, God helping me.

In Philadelphia, Harriet supported herself as a housekeeper, scrubwoman, and laundress. She reveled in the freedom of earning her own money and the simple pleasure of being able to change employers at will. But her heart was heavy, and she was always planning her return home to free her other family members.

Her first rescue took place about a year after her own escape and involved the escape of her sister (or possibly niece) Mary Ann and her two children. Mary Ann's husband was a free black who aided their escape by smuggling the three of them in a boat to Baltimore where Harriet met them and escorted them farther north. The next year she went back for her brother John; in the fall of 1851, she returned for her husband, John Tubman. But John was already living with another woman by then and refused to

Harriet Tubman

come. Harriet was bitterly disappointed. She focused her anger on helping others, escorting ten slaves to freedom in his stead.

Harriet's method of operation on these raids resembled nothing less than an intense military operation, carried out under extremely dangerous conditions. The group usually left on a Saturday night because they would not be missed until Monday morning, and the handbills announcing their escape could not be printed until then. They traveled under darkness, staying off the roads, using swamps and rivers to hide their tracks, because Harriet knew that "running water tells no tales." She paid someone to follow the slave owners and take down the handbills offering rewards for the escapees' capture as fast as the irate owners could post them.

The slaves used various disguises. Boys were dressed as girls. Young women were dressed as old women or as men. Harriet herself was often disguised as an elderly, stooped woman. With her scarred head and her tendency to fall asleep at any time, she was able to deceive many into believing she was harmless.

At times she would be forced to leave the group to secure food or supplies, and she would then communicate with them through song. If their way were clear she would sing:

> Hail, oh hail ye happy spirits
> Death no more shall make you fear
> No grief nor sorrow, pain nor anger
> Shall no more distress you there.

But if there were danger they would hear:

> Moses go down to Egypt
> Till old Pharo' let me go
> Hadn't been for Adam's fall,
> Shouldn't hab died at all.

And they would know to keep to the hiding place until she came for them.

Harriet was an undisputed military leader. She carried weapons, usually a revolver and a rifle, and was not above using them. Once the journey began, she was uncompromising with those who were frightened and wanted to turn back. There was no remedy but force, she later told her biographer, and she was not above pointing a pistol at a whimpering slave's head and commanding him to "go on or die." Although she could be caring and sympathetic, she refused to let one person betray the rest simply because of cowardice or fear.

Harriet's courage came from a deep faith that she was doing God's work, and He would protect her. She told Sarah Bradford, "Don't I tell you Missus 'twan't me, 'twas de Lord. Jes so long as he wanted to use me he would take care of me, an' when he didn't want me no longer I was ready to go. I always tole him, I'm gwine hole stiddy on to you and you've got to see me through."

The people began to call her Moses, and her reputation for executing daring rescues spread far and wide. In 1857 she smuggled out her own parents, a feat that was more dangerous than most because they were aged and needed to be transported by wagon. By the end of 1857, all of her family was free except for one sister and her children whom she was never successful in rescuing.

Harriet usually conducted her charges up through northern Delaware into Pennsylvania, over the Mason-Dixon Line from slave territory to free. She never learned to read or write, but she could remember the most circuitous of routes. One well-traveled route led through New Jersey on into New York City. Once she reached New York, she knew she was in friendlier territory. Although slave catchers still threatened fugitives, the state had emancipated its slaves in 1827.

The Underground Railroad was well established throughout New York State. From New York City, the fugitives could pass relatively safely by foot or stagecoach, or even by boat on the Hudson River to Albany, on up to Troy, across the western part of the state to Syracuse and Rochester, and finally on to freedom in Canada. In his 1943 biography of Harriet, *Harriet Tubman*, Earl Conrad describes that area:

> If Boston was the agitational center for New England, then Central New York was the stage for the Empire State. Abolition and women's suffrage thrived, as busy organizations raised their protests constantly and rooted the anti-slavery mood into the hearts of thousands. Auburn, the home of William H. Seward, was a hive for the Underground, as well as a publishing center for Abolitionist literature. . . . Central New York was the sphere of Seward, Smith and Douglass, of Susan Anthony and Elizabeth Cady Stanton; and a rallying ground for the parliamentary struggle among Eastern anti-slavers.

As remarkable as her accomplishments were, Harriet could never have done it alone. She relied on many others, both black and white, who offered food, shelter, clothing, and transportation along the way. In Philadelphia, William Still formed one of the first vigilance committees to aid slaves in their flight to freedom. In Peterboro, New York, Harriet often found shelter in the home of reformer and philanthropist Gerrit Smith, cousin to Elizabeth Cady Stanton. But by far the most influential of Harriet's friends was William H. Seward, who lived in Auburn, New York.

William H. Seward was a prominent statesman who served as governor of New York State from 1839 to 1843 and was elected to the United States Senate in 1848. He was a staunch abolitionist who felt slavery was morally reprehensible. Despite the fact that Harriet was a fugitive from her owners in the South, in 1857 he sold her property in Auburn, New York, on which to settle her family and lent her the money to buy it. This was momentous. Ever since the Supreme Court's Dred Scott Decision, which stated, "slaves are not citizens of any state or of the United States," it was almost impossible for blacks to buy property, but Seward helped her anyway.

Seward lost a bid for the presidency in 1860, but he would soon serve as secretary of state under President Lincoln. Thanks to William H. Seward, Harriet was able to make Auburn a permanent home for herself and her parents. And through Seward, Harriet met a man who was as bold and determined to see an end to slavery as she was—John Brown.

John Brown was born in Connecticut in 1800 and had spent most of his adult life fighting against the evils of slavery. In 1857 he devised a plan to free southern slaves by force and to establish settlements for them in the mountains of Virginia. John Brown called Harriet "The General" and was one of her greatest admirers. Harriet in turn was greatly impressed by Brown's bravery and dedication. She met him in Boston in the winter of 1858 and discussed plans to recruit men to join his cause.

To support these plans he needed arms, so in 1859 he led a raid on the U.S. arsenal in Harpers Ferry, Virginia (now West Virginia). His forces were eventually overcome by U.S. marines, and most of his men were killed, including two of his sons. John Brown was later hanged for treason, but his actions helped precipitate the conflict that would be called the "War Between the States." Harriet had not taken an active part in the raid but had enlisted men to help and had shared with Brown what information she could about the routes of the Underground Railroad.

Times were dangerous for Harriet. Throughout 1859 she had been speaking publicly throughout the North to raise funds to continue her work and to support her parents, though there was still a reward offered for her capture. Some accounts list it as anywhere from twelve thousand to forty thousand dollars. And after the raid at Harper's Ferry, it was rumored that she had assisted John Brown with money and recruits. It was time for her to lay low for a while. She made her last foray to rescue a party of slaves in December 1860, while rumors of the coming war rumbled about her. Finally her friends convinced her to flee to Canada, where slavery was illegal, and she would be safe.

When the Civil War finally began in 1861, Harriet came down from Canada and volunteered to help the Union forces in South Carolina, working as a cook and a nurse and acting as a liaison between the freed slaves and the Union forces. Before long her duties became as covert and dangerous as her former forays to rescue slaves, as her skills at espionage and scouting were again called on.

Harriet knew how to slip through the countryside undetected. She often used the disguise of a nondescript black woman to slip behind enemy lines and spy for the Union forces. In 1863, when blacks were finally allowed to join the military, she organized a corps of scouts and river pilots who conducted daring intelligence operations throughout the region. Under the command of Colonel James Montgomery, she successfully led a band of African-American soldiers behind enemy lines, and in the Battle of Fort Wagner, she herself came under fire from enemy troops along with the heroic 54th Massachusetts Infantry, the Union army's celebrated black regiment.

When the Civil War was over, Harriet returned to Auburn, New York, to rest from her battles and continue caring for her aged parents. For thirty-five years she would struggle unsuccessfully to obtain a government pension for her years of active service during the war. In 1867 her husband, John, died, and she eventually married again to a Civil War veteran named Nelson Davis, a black man twenty-two years her junior. It was only after his death that she was granted a government pension as his widow—the sum of eight dollars a month. (It was finally increased to twenty dollars a month in 1899 because of her service to her country.)

In her later years Harriet Tubman worked for women's suffrage and opened a home for aged and infirm blacks in Auburn. She died there March 10, 1913, and a local unit of Civil War veterans fired a volley over her grave as a tribute.

Before Martin Luther King Jr. made the phrase famous, Harriet Tubman "had a dream"—the dream of freedom and equality for all. She suffered abuse and braved terrifying conditions to make this dream a reality for herself and her family. She cared for and battled beside Union soldiers of both races during the Civil War, and when the war was over, she returned home to found a home for the poorest and sickest of her people.

During nineteen trips into slave territory, she shepherded over three hundred slaves to freedom and never lost a single one. History has been slow to honor her, but there is talk of listing five sites in Auburn on the National Register of Historic Places, including her house and the church in which she worshipped. Two postage stamps have been issued to commemorate her, one in 1978, the other in 1995. The governor of New York is considering naming March 10, the day she died, as Harriet Tubman Day in the state.

Harriet would probably be honored by such acclaim, but more than honor she wished for freedom for her people, first from slavery, later from want. And she showed at least a small measure of pride in her accomplishments toward these goals when she told a gathering of suffragists in the 1890s, "I was the conductor of the Underground Railroad for eight years, and I can say what most conductors can't say—I never ran my train off the track and I never lost a passenger."

EMILY WARREN ROEBLING
1843–1903

An Unlikely Bridge Builder

*T*he rooster flapped and squawked and tried to break free. It was not used to being confined to a cage and certainly had never ridden in a victoria carriage before. But the well-dressed lady who held its cage on her lap was not about to release it, and for a time at least, freedom for the rooster was just a distant dream.

The lady in the carriage, Emily Warren Roebling, was well acquainted with distant dreams. She and her husband, Washington, had been working on one for fourteen years—the building of the Brooklyn Bridge over the East River, and it was coming to fruition at last. She carried the caged rooster on her lap as a symbol of victory—victory over illness, adversity, political wrangling, financial problems, and the fierce and punishing force of the East River. The bridge had claimed the life of her father-in-law and the health of her husband. During its construction more than twenty other men had lost their lives; her own had been turned upside down. Without quite knowing how, she had changed from a retiring new wife and mother to a respected civil engineer, credited with much of the success of the massive project.

Emily Warren Roebling

The carriage wound its way from her house in Brooklyn up and over the approach, then out onto the bridge itself. Hers was the first carriage ever driven across the bridge, and history was written with every roll of the wheels. Her hard work and devotion to both the bridge and her husband had secured this special privilege. The workers lining her route cheered her and raised their hats in salute. Behind her, she knew her husband was watching from the window of their home. Beneath her, the East River flowed. Farther north it would meet with the mighty Hudson River, another river that had played an important role in Emily's life.

The Hudson River has always been a force to be reckoned with in Cold Spring, New York, the small village where Emily Warren was born on September 23, 1843. Through her youth she would share her community's concerns about the river—a rise in the summer from too much rain or an impending freeze-over during a long, cold winter. As a child in Cold Spring, she often fell asleep to the lonely call of riverboat whistles as the majestic side-wheelers made their way up the Hudson and down. Sometimes they stopped at the dock at the foot of Main Street, and the whole town would be infused with excitement.

Emily was the second to youngest of twelve children born to Sylvanus Warren and his wife, Phebe Lickley. Of the twelve, only six survived. The Warrens were not wealthy, but they had achieved some prominence in the Putnam Valley region of New York. Emily's father served in the New York State Assembly and counted as a close personal friend the writer Washington Irving, author of such classic tales as "The Legend of Sleepy Hollow" and "Rip Van Winkle." Part of the family's financial support came from Sylvanus Warren's investments in the West Point Foundry, where the famous Parrott gun was manufactured, a gun that later played an important role in the Civil War. Although there is little known about her childhood, it can be imagined that life on the banks of the Hudson in the small town of Cold Spring offered the usual winter pleasures of ice-skating and sleigh riding. In the summer Emily rode horses and was considered an excellent horsewoman.

She was especially close to her brother, Gouverneur Kemble Warren, called G. K., eldest of the six surviving children. G. K. attended West Point and graduated second in his class. Fourteen years older than Emily, he was to her a wonderfully dashing and romantic figure. He explored the Black Hills, fought the Sioux, and ran expeditions that mapped the states of Nebraska and North and South Dakota. During the Civil War he rose to the rank of general, was in command of the 5th Corp of the Army of the Potomac, and fought at the Battle of Gettysburg.

When their father died, Emily was just sixteen, and G. K. took over much of Emily's care, as well as that of his other brothers and sisters. He had an intimate interest in their lives and offered to pay for their education. In 1858 he enrolled Emily in the Georgetown Visitation Convent in Washington, D.C., where she studied a variety of subjects, including geology, history, art, and music. She had a bright and lively intellect, showing a particular interest in science. But G. K. Warren did more for his sister than see that she was cared for and well educated. He introduced her to his aide and friend, Washington Roebling.

Washington Roebling was the son of the well-known engineer John A. Roebling, who had been born in Germany and immigrated to the United States as a young man. John A. Roebling established a company that was one of the first to manufacture rope from wire. He was famous for his construction of a suspension bridge over the Niagara River and the Allegheny suspension bridge in Pittsburgh, Pennsylvania. Washington Roebling followed in his father's footsteps and studied engineering at Rensselaer

Polytechnic Institute in Troy, New York, graduating in 1857. In April 1861 he enlisted in the Army and two years later was assigned to the staff of General G. K. Warren.

In 1864, even though the Civil War was raging, Emily convinced her family to allow her to visit her brother at his encampment in Virginia, and it was there that she was introduced to young Washington Roebling. They met at a military ball, and it seemed that for Washington at least it was love at first sight. He later wrote to his sister that Emily had "captured your brother Washy's heart at last." They were married in Cold Spring on January 18, 1865, in a double ceremony with Emily's brother Edgar and his fiancée, Cornelia Barrows.

The next few years marked a halcyon time for the newlyweds. They lived first in Cincinnati, where Washington was assisting his father with the building of a bridge between Cincinnati and Covington, Kentucky. In 1867 Washington's father sent him to Europe to study the construction of pneumatic caissons and invited Emily, who was by this time expecting their first child, to go along. Their son, John, was born in November 1867 in the German town of Muhlhausen, ancestral home of the Roebling family. Emily's health was at first threatened by a serious fall sustained before the birth, but she eventually recovered. The small family returned home in March 1868 to face the greatest challenge of their lives—the building of the Brooklyn Bridge.

John A. Roebling had long held the dream of building a bridge over the East River that would connect Brooklyn, then a separate city, to the lower part of the island of Manhattan, the center of commerce and finance. Without a bridge the only way to travel across was by boat or ferry, a method that was often thwarted by fog, ice, or raging tides. But many thought such a bridge to be an impossible dream. After all it would have to span 2,500 feet from shore to shore and be built high enough for ships to pass under. No one knew how to build such a bridge. No one, that is, except John A. Roebling.

In 1857 John wrote to Horace Greely, editor of the *New York Tribune*, voicing his opinion on the benefits of a bridge to promote commerce and communication between the two cities. He wrote to businessmen and politicians in New York and Brooklyn, trying to convince them of the economic necessity of the bridge. But no one believed it was feasible. It wasn't until the frigid winter of 1867–68, when ice choked the East River and made passage by boat and ferry almost impossible, that people finally began to take the idea seriously. A bill was finally passed by the New York State legislature to fund the project, and construction of the bridge began. Its cost was estimated at seven million dollars.

John A. Roebling planned a suspension bridge that would be the longest in the world, crossing over the East River in a single span. Its roadway would be suspended from four huge cables that would in turn be supported by two towers, each 276.5 feet tall. When the cables passed over the towers, their ends would be secured by two huge stone anchorages, one on the New York side and one on the Brooklyn side, each the size of a city block. The bridge's total length would be over 1 mile, and its towers would be taller than anything else on the New York City skyline, except for the Trinity Church spire.

The bridge would not just be practical, it would be beautiful as well, with tall, graceful arches for traffic to pass through and a unique elevated promenade for pedestrians to enjoy. And, in a bold and innovative stroke, John A. Roebling declared the bridge would be made of steel instead of iron.

John A. Roebling had many grand dreams for his bridge, but he did not live to see any of them realized. One day while waiting for the ferry on the Brooklyn side of the river, his foot slipped and was crushed against the piling by the ferry as it docked. He developed tetanus, and after weeks of extreme suffering, he died on July 22, 1869.

Emily and her father-in-law had enjoyed a close relationship based on mutual respect. After the birth of her son in Germany, she had written him that the boy would be named after him, expressing her hopes that he "may not prove unworthy of the name." Both she and her husband were devastated, not only by John A. Roebling's death, but also by the enormous responsibility that now lay on his son Washington's slender shoulders. Washington had been his father's assistant on the bridge project. He now had to take over completion of the project himself. What no one could foresee at the time was how much of that responsibility would fall not only on Washington's shoulders, but on those of his young wife Emily as well.

Washington Roebling began work on the bridge almost immediately, beginning with the construction of the caissons, huge upside-down wood-and-iron boxes to be lowered into the water. The bridge's towers would be supported by two massive concrete foundations, and those foundations would be constructed deep in the water through the use of the caissons. Compressed air would be continually pumped into the caissons to force the water out. The builders would work inside these caissons, digging down to reach the river's bedrock. Rocks and debris would be removed through water-filled shafts. Once bedrock was reached, the caissons would be filled with concrete to become the foundations for the bridge's towers.

Work in the caissons was dirty, hot, and dangerous. The threat of fire was greater in compressed air, and several fires delayed the work. As the men dug deeper, and the caissons inched closer to the riverbed, the air pressure inside increased, making it more and more difficult to breathe and work. And as the caissons went lower, the towers of limestone and granite that would support the bridge's cables were built on top of them, increasing the pressure even more.

The workers traveled from the surface of the river down into the caissons through a system of air locks that were supposed to allow their bodies to become gradually accustomed to the changes in air pressure. If the men did not spend enough time in the air locks, nitrogen bubbles would form in their blood, and they would develop the dreaded caisson disease, later known as "the bends." Most of the workers felt some symptoms of the sickness, which included painful cramps, dizziness, and paralysis; some died from it.

Washington himself suffered an attack of caisson disease in December of 1870 when fire broke out during the construction of the Brooklyn caisson, and he found himself traveling too rapidly up and down from the surface to the caisson. During the construction of the New York caisson, he again traveled up and down through the locks frequently, testing the riverbed and making crucial decisions about the construction. During the next several weeks, the attacks became more frequent and severe. Finally, by December 1872 he was unable to return to the worksite at all.

Both the Roeblings were distraught by this development. "At first I thought I would succumb," said Washington later, "but I had a strong tower to lean upon, my wife, a woman of infinite tact and wisest counsel."

Emily's skills as a diplomat were called into play almost immediately, as her first job was to convince the president of the New York Bridge Company, Henry C. Murphy, that Washington could continue his duties as chief engineer of the project despite his illness. She assured Murphy that Washington was ill, but that he would be able to resume his position in the spring. Fortunately Murphy agreed to keep him on as chief engineer, so with Emily's assistance Washington began to write a comprehensive set of longhand instructions for the completion of the bridge, including detailed sketches and diagrams. Emily relayed messages and instructions to the assistant engineers at the site who were supervising the construction in his absence. But by the spring, it was obvious that Washington's health was not improving. He and Emily left for Germany for a six-month leave of absence that they hoped would help him recover.

But when they returned, Washington's health was still poor. Following his doctor's recommendation of continued rest, Washington and his family returned to the family home in Trenton, New Jersey, where they lived for the next three years. Work on the bridge continued, supervised by the assistant engineers at the site and by Washington's daily letters, which, as his eyesight failed, Emily transcribed and wrote for him.

The massive towers and their anchorages were completed in 1876, and work was begun on the spinning of the steel cables. The Roeblings returned to Brooklyn, moving into a house in Brooklyn Heights that was only a half mile from the bridge. Its rear windows offered a wonderful, unobstructed view of the bridge from one end to the other. It was from this window that Washington would supervise the completion of the project.

But he would not do it alone. In addition to poor eyesight, he suffered from severe headaches and nervous exhaustion and was unable to tolerate any company other than Emily's. It was she who continued to take his dictation and read to him any correspondence that he received. She became extremely knowledgeable in mathematics and engineering and comfortably conversant with such topics as catenary curves, stress analysis, and the intricacies of cable construction. There were those who suspected that she had actually taken over many of the duties of chief engineer. An article in the *New York Times* in May 1883 illustrates this perfectly, reporting the words of a "gentlemen well-acquainted with the family":

> When bids for the steel and iron work for the structure were advertised for three or four years ago it was found that entirely new shapes would be required, such as no mill was then making. This necessitated new patterns and representatives of the mills desiring to bid went to New York to consult with Mr. Roebling. Their surprise was great when Mrs. Roebling sat down with them, and by her knowledge of engineering, helped them out with their patterns and cleared away difficulties that had for weeks been puzzling their brains.

Such a concept was almost impossible for most people to believe. That a Victorian wife and mother might have the mental capacity to understand such intricate concepts was difficult enough to believe. Women's brains, it was commonly held at the time, were simply not capable of comprehending such complex ideas. But for a woman to even partially assume the duties of chief engineer of one of the greatest monuments ever built was totally inconceivable. Emily was well aware of the fact that if the scope of her assistance to her husband's work were to be known, public confidence in the project would be eroded, and after so many years, the entire project might be compromised. Indeed, if it were true that she had taken on many of the duties of chief engineer, it would add further proof to the rumors that Washington had finally lost not only his physical capabilities, but his mind as well.

Every single correspondence that went to the worksite was in Emily's hand, and eventually many of the letters to the house came addressed directly to her. She shielded her husband from the strain of visitors, meeting with them herself and answering their questions with such supreme confidence that many left the house convinced they had met with the chief engineer after all.

In 1881 the newly elected mayor of Brooklyn, Seth Low, attempted to have Washington fired as chief engineer, and New York newspapers called for his removal for inability to perform the job. After all he had not visited the construction site since December 1872, and rumors still persisted that Emily had taken over the job of chief engineer completely. Emily was constantly called on to defend her husband and to act as intermediary between these battling groups. In 1882 she became the first woman to speak before the American Society of Civil Engineers, eloquently explaining to its members why she believed Washington should not be replaced as chief engineer.

Emily continued to visit the worksite daily, carrying her husband's instructions to the crew, meeting with the trustees of the New York Bridge Company, discussing supplies and deadlines with contractors and vendors. She was quite literally her husband's "eyes, his ears, his good right arm." It was no surprise, given her gifted intelligence and day-to-day exposure to the project, that she developed a keen insight into its problems and development. As the years passed, she won the respect and admiration of everyone associated with the project.

By 1883 the bridge was almost finished. It was time to test the roadway with a carriage. Washington asked that Emily have the honor of being the first to cross. As she drove across the bridge from one end to the other, the caged rooster perched on her lap, the cheers from the workmen and bystanders were as much for her as they were for her husband and father-in-law. All the Roeblings had built an outstandingly beautiful bridge.

The Brooklyn Bridge formally opened on May 24, 1883. President Chester A. Arthur attended the opening ceremonies, as did scores of dignitaries. Washington watched from his window as

PHOTO BY ANTONIA PETRASH

The Brooklyn Bridge today

Emily and their son John walked across the bridge from the Brooklyn side to meet the president and his party coming from the New York side. Warships in the river below fired a salute. A band played "Hail to the Chief." Church bells pealed, and thousands of invited guests cheered and applauded. Later that night Emily and Washington held a party for hundreds, including President Arthur, and fireworks celebrating the completion of the bridge lit the New York City sky. The bridge was considered to be the greatest engineering feat in the history of the United States.

During the fourteen years that she had worked with her husband on the building of the Brooklyn Bridge, Emily's life had been spent in an almost entirely male circle. Now with the bridge finished, she was free to develop interests that were more traditionally associated with women. Her son graduated from Rensselaer Polytechnic Institute in 1888 and was married the following year, thus freeing her from many traditional family duties. She became active in the Federation of Women's Clubs, joining the Sorosis Club and the Daughters of the American Revolution. In 1899 she took on another immense challenge and enrolled in New York University Woman's Law Class. Although not the equivalent of a full-time law school, it offered instruction in such matters as contracts and property law and was designed to acquaint women with the intricacies of the American legal system. Emily devoted herself to the course with her usual passion and graduated with high honors, winning an award of fifty dollars for her final essay, entitled "A Wife's Disabilities," which made an eloquent plea for equal rights for women before the law.

She spent the remainder of her life lecturing, writing, and enjoying life with her son, his wife, and her two grandsons. She became ill in 1902 and died on February 28, 1903. She was fifty-eight years old.

Emily Warren Roebling had been born in a time of limited expectations for women, when serving home and family were considered to be their most appropriate and rewarding career. To indulge oneself in grandiose ideas of entering a profession was considered gauche and unladylike, totally beneath society's expectations of proper behavior. Emily began life fully intending to honor these tenets.

But life demanded more of her. Her husband's ill health offered her an unexpected opportunity to put her intelligence to practical use and to prove that women certainly could be as successful at scientific and technical endeavors as men could. The Brooklyn Bridge might have been the dream of John and Washington Roebling, but without Emily's assistance Washington Roebling never could have completed the job.

A prominent plaque on the east tower of the bridge gives testament to this fact today. Emily would have been pleased by its inscription:

The Builders of the Bridge
Dedicated to the Memory of
Emily Warren Roebling
1843–1903
whose faith and courage helped her stricken husband
Col. Washington A. Roebling, C.E.
1837–1926
complete the construction of this bridge
from the plans of his father
John A. Roebling, C.E.
1806–1869
who gave his life to the bridge

"BACK OF EVERY GREAT WORK WE CAN FIND

THE SELF-SACRIFICING DEVOTION OF A WOMAN."

PHOTO BY DENTON TAYLOR/www.dentontaylor.com

Brooklyn Bridge plaque honoring the Roeblings

KATHARINE BEMENT DAVIS
1860–1935

Prison Reformer

The sound of breaking glass reverberated in the Philadelphia air as every single window in the building was reduced to shards of glass. The perpetrator moved steadily and methodically from room to room before anyone could stop her, until not a single window was left intact, and the building was rendered uninhabitable.

Katharine Bement Davis was generally a law-abiding young woman, an unlikely mastermind of such destruction, but she had broken things before, chiefly stereotypical ideas about what women could and could not do. And she would break things in the future, including barriers to the employment of women in the male-dominated field of prison management and penal reform. Katharine Bement Davis would become the first woman in New York City's history to run a major municipal agency. She would be in charge of 5,500 inmates and command 650 uniform and civilian employees and a two-million-dollar annual budget. She would become the first woman to run for public office, even before her sex had been awarded the right to vote!

Katharine Bement Davis

But right now as the head resident and director of day-to-day activities of the College Settlement House in Philadelphia, she was breaking all the windows in a condemned tenement house. Without windows the Settlement House's benefactors could not force poor families to live in the building. They would be compelled to find better housing for them.

Katharine Bement Davis herself was not poor. She was born in Buffalo, New York, on January 15, 1860, the oldest of five children—three girls and two boys. Her mother was Frances Bement, daughter of an ardent feminist and suffragist. Her father, Oscar Bill Davis, was a manager for the Bradstreet Company, a precursor to Dun and Bradstreet. Both parents traced their American origins to the 1600s, both counting Ethan Allen among their ancestors. When Katharine was three years old, the family moved to Dunkirk, New York, and later, when she was seventeen, to Rochester.

The Davis's home life was warm and happy. Her father was an ardent believer in the benefits of education for all his children, including the girls, and instruction in music, dancing, and art complemented their formal studies. Her family was neither rich nor poor, and Katharine was comfortable with their middle-class status. She liked to relate that her father provided generously for them all, but that she did not ever "suffer from an overabundance of money."

Katharine enjoyed a close relationship with her maternal grandmother, who before the Civil War had agitated for the abolition of slavery and later for suffrage and women's rights. Rhoda Denison Bement had attended the historic Seneca Falls Women's Rights Convention organized by Lucretia Mott and Elizabeth Cady Stanton in 1848. She was an ardent believer in social change for the betterment of all members of society, but especially for women. Katharine would remember lively discussions about social reform with her grandmother; they were an influence that Katharine would draw from in the future.

Katharine attended the Rochester Free Academy, a public high school, where she did well in mathematics and found the sciences, especially chemistry, most fascinating. She was encouraged by her teachers to seek higher education but was disappointed when a reversal in her father's economic fortunes prevented her from attending college.

Instead of complaining she went to work teaching science at Dunkirk High School. But Katharine never gave up her dream of attending college. During the day she taught botany, geology, and chemistry to young girls. At night and on weekends, she took college courses and saved her salary. It was difficult enough for a young woman to attend college, even more difficult for one with little money. Finally, after ten years of working and saving, she won advanced placement at Vassar College. She left her teaching position and entered the college as a junior. She was thirty years old.

Vassar itself was only twenty-five years old when Katharine attended, but it had already established a reputation for excellence in the fields of science, nutrition, and food chemistry—all subjects that Katharine was drawn to and excelled at. When she graduated with honors two years later, she taught briefly at Brooklyn Heights Seminary for Girls, while taking graduate courses in food chemistry at Columbia University. But she discovered that she was no longer content to teach science to young women. Following the ideals of her grandmother, she was determined to use her education to solve the social and economic problems of society.

An opportunity to do just that arose in the spring of 1893 when she was appointed director of a model workingman's home, part of an exhibit to be put on by New York State at the World's Columbian Exposition in Chicago. The exposition sought to demonstrate not only what had been accomplished in the past four hundred years in America, but what exciting innovations also could be expected in the future. The crowds who attended the exposition were dazzled by electrified streetcars, an elevated railway, and a day-care center for infants. Everything was new and daring, designed to offer innovative examples of life in the next century.

Katharine seized upon her new job with delight. Architects at Pratt Institute in Brooklyn drew up plans for the actual house, but she planned just about everything else. She purchased every single item for the "family," from the biscuit cutter for three cents to the large rocker in the living room for three dollars. The exhibit was designed to show over a twenty-eight-day period how a working-man's family of five could live comfortably on $500 a year. Katharine planned meticulous menus, calculated nutritional and caloric needs for every family member, and tracked the cost of everything down to the penny. Katharine's "family" carried out all their daily chores and activities in the presence of from 500 to 2,000 fair visitors daily in a house with many modern innovations, including indoor plumbing and generous closet space.

The success of the exhibit led to the offer of a position as head resident at the St. Mary's Street College Settlement House in Philadelphia. One of the first settlement houses in the United States, the College Settlement House had been founded in 1892.

Settlement houses were charitable institutions established to provide social services to those in need, including immigrants. Conditions in the late nineteenth century were not unlike conditions faced by the urban poor in major cities today. The growth of modern industry led many to migrate from a rural to an urban environment. There was a tremendous surge of immigration, with many Irish fleeing from the potato famine in Ireland, as an example. As the century came to an end, the separation of social classes became more pronounced, with many people developing an aversion to immigrants and to the urban poor who poured into the cities and taxed their services.

Because one of the goals of the settlement program was to improve housing conditions for working families, Katharine's experience developing the workingman's home at the exposition proved invaluable. During the course of her tenure at College Settlement House, she created four model tenement apartments, much like the exposition exhibit, and, as shown by her window-smashing experiment, she refused to allow poor families to live in substandard conditions. The College Settlement House developed a kindergarten for the education of immigrant and minority children and began a vigorous campaign for local school improvement. It offered music lessons, planted gardens, and taught English.

The settlement house experience confirmed in Katharine a commitment to social reform, and she never lost her own desire for further education. In 1897, at the age of thirty-seven, she resigned her position to study for a doctoral degree in political economics at the University of Chicago.

At the end of the nineteenth century, society was gradually coming to accept the idea of advanced education for women. Many middle- and upper-class women were entering colleges and universities to seek undergraduate and graduate degrees; nearly eight times as many women earned Ph.D.s in the 1890s as in all the decades before.

Katharine came to the university to study economics because she believed that a judicious application of sound economic practice could benefit society as a whole, especially women. She saw economics and politics as inextricably linked. Her mentor at the university was Thorstein Veblen, who taught political economics and encouraged his students to enlarge their understanding of human behavior through the study of anthropology. But other professors influenced her there as well. Professor Albion Small taught her the importance of conducting objective research when trying to solve social problems. J. Laurence Laughlin impressed on her the importance of scientific knowledge when applied to social reform. Katharine certainly did not agree with all her professors' views, but she was able to distill from these differing points of view her own unique formulas and ideas, which would serve her well in the future.

In 1898 Katharine received a fellowship from the New England Women's Educational Association and set out for Europe to study the living conditions of women farm laborers in Bohemia. She wanted to compare their standard of living with that of Czech immigrants who had settled in Chicago. As she had at College Settlement House, Katharine preferred to live among the people whom she was studying to learn first-hand the problems they faced. She learned their language and shared their lives.

Czech women routinely performed heavy farm labor for eight hours a day in the winter and twelve to fourteen hours a day in the summer, but received one-third less in wages than men performing the same tasks. Far from being dull-witted or lazy, a common racist view of peasants, Katharine found that it was a history of exploitive child labor that had stunted their development and thus had condemned them to a life of servitude. Relying on personal observation, an exhaustive study of public records, and interviews with workers and estate owners, she was able to construct a groundbreaking analysis of the conditions in that region. Later she would apply what she learned in Bohemia to her work in prison reform, never forgetting the effects that poor economic conditions and racist and sexist prejudices could have on women's lives.

Katharine Davis graduated with a doctorate in political economy in June 1900. During the entire nineteenth century, only fifteen women achieved that distinction and five of them were from the University of Chicago. She was now an ordained social scientist and was looking forward to translating those scientific principles she had taken such pains to master into potential agents for social change.

But an advanced degree in no way guaranteed entry into a profession, many of which were still dominated by men. Women university professors were rare; within the next few years, they would become rarer still. Thankfully Katharine did not have a strong desire to return to teaching. Instead another job presented itself, one for which her interest in contemporary social problems would make her the perfect candidate.

In March 1900 Josephine Shaw Lowell, a noted New York prison reformer, contacted the University of Chicago's dean of women, Marion Talbot, to ask if Talbot knew of any "suitable" college women who might be interested in the position of superintendent of a new women's reformatory that was to open soon in New York. Talbot immediately thought of Katharine Davis and suggested her for the job. Katharine passed the civil service test easily, and in 1901 became superintendent of the New York State Reformatory for Women at Bedford Hills.

It seemed Katharine Davis had been preparing for this job her entire life. She had taught young girls and had worked with poor immigrant women at the settlement house. She had seen first hand the tragic consequences of poverty and low social class in the fields of Czechoslovakia. She herself had experienced political and professional ostracism in the academic world simply because she was a woman. All of these factors combined to make her the perfect candidate for the superintendent of a women's prison.

The women's reformatory at Bedford Hills was only the third reformatory established for women in New York and was founded upon the principle of reform rather than incarceration. Prisoners came from New York City, Long Island, and Westchester County.

Their crimes were primarily petty larceny, drunkenness, and prostitution. Most lived in cottages, some with nurseries for children under the age of two. Many of the cottages had gardens and kitchens. Inmates cooked meals for their fellow prisoners under the watchful eye of the matrons. Katharine liked to compare the prison to an educational institution. Inmates were encouraged to govern themselves. Released prisoners were referred to as "graduates."

Katharine broke with prison tradition almost immediately. While men were taught practical trades in prison, women were usually taught domestic skills that only prepared them to work as servants. But Katharine knew that women were capable of much more than that. "Every woman is not adapted to domestic service any more than is every man to the trade of tailor," she asserted. In addition to the traditional skills of cooking and canning, the women were taught skills that would help them to find jobs on release, skills such as basket weaving and working in a steam laundry. Convinced that the prison experience could make a positive impact in these women's lives, Katharine began to develop school programs as well.

She believed that working outdoors in the fresh air helped inmates build both physical strength and pride of accomplishment. When the prison buildings needed improvement, she learned how to pour concrete herself then taught the skill to the inmates. Prisoners graded and seeded lawns, shoveled snow, ran the reformatory farm, and learned to keep records of their own accounts.

Katharine was one of the first to promote the idea that whatever their race or ethnic background, women's criminal activity usually derived from low wages and the lack of opportunity for adequate education and employment rather than an inborn tendency toward crime. She was against racial segregation, an unpopular stance at a time when such segregation in prisons was routine.

In 1912 she convinced philanthropist John Davis to fund a scientific study that later led to the establishment of the Bureau of Social Hygiene at Bedford Hills. The bureau grew from Katharine's continued concern for prisoners who seemed impervious to reform and who returned again and again to criminal life, especially to prostitution. She hoped that bringing scientific experts together to examine these women might help to find ways to rehabilitate them.

Her studies showed that the majority of the young women who became prostitutes were white, native-born Americans, and that most of those women had a family history that included insanity and disease. With information gained from research at the bureau, Katharine was able to institute programs for special medical attention for sex offenders and programs to separate the potentially reformable inmates from more hardened criminals. Troubled inmates were often difficult to manage, and she sometimes had to admit that some seemed almost impossible to reform.

In 1914, New York City's Reform Mayor John Mitchel offered Katharine a cabinet position in city government as commissioner of corrections. She would be the first woman to hold such a post. As commissioner, Katharine could apply her theories of social reform to over five thousand inmates in nine city prisons and jails. Although she was reluctant to leave Bedford Hills, she accepted the position on January 1, 1914. She was fifty-three years old.

One of her first acts was to abolish the wearing of striped uniforms because she believed "half the degradation and sulleness of prisoners is a result of their hideous stripes." She also halted the practice of allowing public sightseeing tours of the jails. She felt it was degrading for inmates to be "gazed upon like wild beasts in cages."

She worked to suppress narcotic peddling in the prisons and in 1914 quelled a serious riot by the prisoners of Blackwell Island.

She also established a farm colony for boys in Orange County where the young men could work in the open air, improved food and medical care, offered practical education courses, and tirelessly pressed for better living conditions for the inmates. She sought higher pay and better working conditions for the prison keepers who were entrusted with the prisoners' care.

Katharine's tenure as commissioner of corrections was unfortunately brief. She resigned her position in 1915 to become head of the parole board, another position she thought would offer her an opportunity to help those less fortunate than herself. Indeed, she regarded the job as the most important she had held up to that point in her life.

She contacted businesses and civic and philanthropic groups to secure housing, jobs, and training for released inmates. She actively worked with legislators to draft a law for indeterminate sentencing, a process that allowed the judge to determine the sentence the prisoner would receive within a certain range allowed by law. In this way the possibility of parole could be used as an incentive for inmate rehabilitation. The indeterminate sentencing structure was used by the city of New York for over fifty years, with hundreds of thousands of prisoners being offered the benefit of rehabilitative assistance.

Katharine never forgot the ideals her suffragist grandmother had instilled in her and worked steadily to achieve the vote for women. She even became a candidate herself, running briefly in 1914 as the Women's Suffrage Party's candidate for delegate-at-large, the first women ever to run for statewide office. She lost.

In 1917 Mayor Mitchel lost a bid for reelection, and Katharine left her post as head of the parole board to work full-time for the Rockefeller Bureau of Social Hygiene. Under her direction the bureau continued to investigate the root of social problems, especially those of prostitutes and other women who turned to lives of crime on the city streets.

While continuing her research on criminal activity, Katharine turned to researching sexual behavior. "Nice" women didn't discuss sex in the early 1920s, especially those who had never married. But not only did Katharine discuss it, she surveyed the sexual practices of over two thousand married and unmarried women, asking intimate questions no one had dared ask before. Women responded to her survey with candid answers about such controversial questions as the frequency of the sexual act and the presence or absence of homosexual activity. Her groundbreaking study, *Factors in the Sex Life of Twenty-Two Hundred Women*, was published in 1929. It also included a study of why many professional women chose not to marry, which was particularly ironic, considering that Katharine herself had never done so.

Later years saw her take an active role in the prevention and eradication of venereal disease and narcotics addiction. She finally retired in 1928 and moved to Pacific Grove, California, where she lived with her two sisters until her death in 1935 at the age of seventy-five.

Katharine began her life as a determined and cheerful child, taught by her family to believe in the dual benefits of education and hard work. From her maternal grandmother she developed advanced ideas on social reform, believing from a young age in the benefits of helping those less fortunate. Katharine believed most women turned to crime because of a lack of education or a low economic status. She believed both male and female prisoners deserved to be housed in decent quarters, receive rehabilitation in the form of health care and education, and, in many cases, should be offered the hope of parole. These benefits belonged to all prisoners, regardless of race, nationality, or religious beliefs.

Her life was not without controversy. She was often criticized; her goals were not always realized. But even when faced with disappointments, she never lost her optimistic view that research and education could better society, especially for its poor and uneducated members.

Katharine Bement Davis's work in prison reform improved the lives of men and women in prisons in New York, and her influence was felt throughout the country. Many of those who worked with her continued the reforms and practices she had instituted. Her pioneering sex research increased public awareness of the dangers of sexual promiscuity and venereal disease. But perhaps her greatest achievement was proving that women could achieve the same goals as men. They could earn advanced degrees, run large organizations, conduct advanced research, and contribute important and lasting improvements to society.

In Katharine Bement Davis's long lifetime of achievement, the cost of those few broken windows was money well spent.

MARY BURNETT TALBERT
1866–1923

Advocate of Equality

*T*he Pan American Exposition opened to great fanfare in the city of Buffalo, New York, in May 1901. Planned as an exposition that would "highlight all the Americas—their people, their land, their technology," it took four years to prepare and was visited by over eight million people.

Visitors were dazzled by the ornate, multicolored buildings; the gracious, parklike setting of the grounds; the elaborate Gothic statues. They were awed by exhibitions of the latest technological achievements of their time, especially the Electric Tower, illuminated nightly by thousands of colored bulbs. Fair-goers were also enthralled by the Midway attractions, where they could visit re-created Eskimo and Japanese villages and even float down a canal in a gondola in a replica of the beautiful Italian city of Venice.

The exposition was open from May until November 1901, and the millions of people who attended came away excited by the athletic events and impressed by the technological advances the future promised.

But one woman came away from the exposition neither impressed nor excited but instead saddened and dismayed by what she found there. When African-American activist Mary Burnett Talbert visited the Midway, instead of an exhibit spotlighting the achievements of her race since the Emancipation Proclamation, she saw an exhibit entitled "The Old Plantation Exhibition," with log cabins said to be occupied by "genuine darkey families and their pickaninnies."

Mary Burnett Talbert had campaigned long and hard to have a member of the African-American race appointed to the board of commissioners of the exposition to prevent such an indignity from occurring, but her efforts and those of others had failed. The black community in Buffalo was deeply offended by that exclusion and by what they considered to be a racist exhibit, an exhibit that totally ignored any of the social and educational advances their race had made since the end of the Civil War. Where did one find evidence of the black physicians, clergymen, writers, educators, or inventors? Were blacks always to be thought of as "darkies on the plantation"? Were they always to be judged as ex-slaves and treated with bigotry and disrespect? Even after a token exhibit showing some advances was allowed in another building, the Midway spectacle of blacks living in shanties far overshadowed it.

But if Mary Burnett Talbert was discouraged by the setback of the Pan American Exposition, she did not let it affect her for long. She was used to fighting for equality and freedom for her race, and she felt tremendous pride in the accomplishments of African Americans, especially since they had only recently thrown off the shackles of slavery. In a 1902 essay in *Twentieth Century Negro Literature*, she wrote:

As the hand upon the dial of the nineteenth-century clock pointed to its last figure it showed that the American Negro had ceased to be a thing, a commodity

Mary Burnett Talbert

that could be bought and sold, a mere animal; but was indeed a human being possessing all the qualities of mind and heart that belong to the rest of mankind. . . . From abject serfdom and pauperism he has risen to a plane far above the masses of any race of people.

Mary Burnett was born September 17, 1866, the youngest of the eight children of Cornelius J. Burnett and Carolyn Nichols Burnett. Mary's parents believed in hard work and the value of a good education. Her father was born in 1813 in Fayetteville, North Carolina, and was a barber by trade. Her mother was born in Raleigh, North Carolina, about 1830 and was said to be the great-granddaughter of Richard Nichols, who captured the settlement of New Amsterdam for the English in 1644 and renamed it New York. The family moved to Oberlin, Ohio, where in addition to raising eight children, her mother ran a boarding house and restaurant that catered to students from Oberlin College. Both parents were active in church, first belonging to the Christ Episcopal Church, then later joining the Second Congregational Church, probably because of its active promotion of education for black youth.

Mary attended public schools in Oberlin, studied the piano, and joined her parents at church. Her father was active in politics and was an elected delegate to several Republican conventions. The family's business, political, and religious activities exerted a profound influence on Mary, providing her with a strong foundation from which to grow and flourish and a self-confidence that would enable her to overcome the limitations that were traditionally imposed on her race and gender. From her parents she learned the rewards of service to church and community.

Mary graduated from Oberlin High School at age sixteen and enrolled in a "literary program" at Oberlin College, one of the first colleges to admit African Americans and women. The program was designed to prepare young women to take "their place in society," as it was perceived at the time. From Oberlin she received a degree in 1894 when she was only nineteen years old. While in college she also cultivated friendships with progressive, young, African-American women such as Mary Church Terrell and Hallie Q. Brown, both of whom would spend much of their lives advocating freedom and equality for blacks. Hallie Q. Brown would later write glowingly about Mary in her book *Homespun Heroines:* "Her personality was most charming, her smile an object of beauty. She possessed a kind, thoughtful, generous nature and a ready and versatile tongue and pen."

The paths of these three women would cross many times during their lives as they struggled against the racism that threatened their educational and economic prosperity.

After graduating from college, Mary moved to Arkansas to assume a teaching position in the segregated Little Rock school system, teaching Latin, science, history, and geography. Mary was an excellent teacher, and in 1887 she became assistant principal of Bethel University, the first woman ever to hold the position. She later left Bethel University to become principal of Union High School in Little Rock.

Mary found herself in a unique position in Little Rock. Although she was accorded respect as a leading black educator, her elevated position did not blind her to the inequities and social restrictions faced by others of her race. "Jim Crow" laws were still in place—laws that dictated separation of races in schools, public bathrooms, and restaurants; prohibited interracial marriages; and in many other ways severely restricted the rights of African Americans. Mary attended public events that called attention to such inequities and built a base of support from individuals and organizations that she was to draw on later in her public life.

While she struggled to develop a public life, her personal life was blossoming. Her sister Henrietta had married Buffalo businessman Robert Talbert, and in 1891, keeping it in the family, Mary married William Herbert Talbert, Robert's brother. William Herbert Talbert was also a prominent businessman and was the bookkeeper for the city of Buffalo. The Talbert family had lived in the Buffalo area for many years and was financially well established. Mary gave up her teaching position in Little Rock and moved with her husband to Buffalo. The following year she gave birth to a daughter, Sara, who would be their only child.

In the later 1800s and early 1900s, the African-American population in the city of Buffalo was small compared with that of other northern cities such as Chicago or New York. Because of this, African Americans in Buffalo enjoyed an amiable relationship with the white community. Their employment opportunities were not restricted to the traditional service sector; they also joined professions and established businesses. The Talbert family lived in comfortable homes, and Mary enjoyed the pleasant activities of a life devoted to the responsibilities of family, church, and community. Although a law against married teachers had forced her to officially withdraw from the teaching profession, she opened classes in her church where she taught Sunday school teachers.

But despite this comfortable life, she was well aware of the cultural and economic differences between the less fortunate blacks and the white community. In 1899 she became a charter member of the Phyllis Wheatley Club, an organization named for the famous young, African-American poet, and a Buffalo affiliate of the National Association of Colored Women (NACW).

The NACW had been formed in Washington, D.C., in 1896. The organization arose from the desire of black women to devise social and economic programs that would help their race respond to the challenges of the new century. Mary and other successful black women felt keenly their responsibility to promote racial solidarity while interacting positively with the white community. They believed the twentieth century marked a new day for black women, a day when they would be called on to rise above passivity and take an active role in leading their race.

Blacks were often hampered in their academic development by poor educational systems. NACW members were convinced that a comprehensive education was vital to ensure the inclusion of young African-Americans in professions and businesses. To combat deficient educational systems, they donated the works of black authors to public libraries, encouraged exhibits of black culture, and invited prominent black intellectuals, such as Mary Church Terrell, to speak. The NACW had been impressed with Mary Talbert's challenge to the all-white board of commissioners of the Pan American Exposition and recognized in her a potent ally.

In 1901 Mary Talbert hosted the biennial convention of the NACW in her home. The group attracted widespread press coverage of its convention sessions. In 1901 she was also elected second president of the Phyllis Wheatley Club, and later that year she founded the Christian Culture Congress, a literary society that offered remedial classes in reading and writing, as well as social, musical, and recreational services. The Christian Culture Congress met on Sunday afternoons in the Michigan Avenue Baptist Church. The church rang with the songs of noted choirs and with the stimulating debates and lectures of famous African-American authors such as Booker T. Washington.

In 1905 activist and writer W. E. B. DuBois called together the "talented tenth" of blacks—lawyers, ministers, teachers, and other educated people—to join the Niagara movement, inaugurated at a conference where the rights of blacks and the repeal of the Jim Crow laws was to be discussed. The meeting was to be held in the city of Buffalo, but participants could not find hotel space available anywhere in the city. Some historians claim an Elks convention had taken all the available rooms; others report that no hotel would rent rooms to blacks. Mary was active in the movement and offered her home for the meeting, but it was decided the group would cross over the Niagara River into Canada. They met in Erie, where they issued their "Declaration of Principles," calling for equal voting rights, equality in economic opportunity, freedom of speech and criticism, and the repeal of the Jim Crow laws.

Such a declaration in 1905 was considered radical and revolutionary and brought to light the very different beliefs of two of the great African-American leaders of the day. Booker T. Washington believed that blacks should not worry about social inequities, but should concentrate on moving into the mainstream by working hard and not agitating for change. W. E. B. DuBois wanted immediate social and political equality and felt it could only be obtained through education and social protest.

Mary tried to forge an effective alliance between both groups. The Niagara Movement was a precursor of the National Association for the Advancement of Colored People (NAACP), which was established in 1909 in New York City. In 1910 under Mary's direction, the Phyllis Wheatley Club invited the newly developed NAACP to form a chapter in Buffalo.

Mary's passion for racial equality drew national attention in 1916 when she was elected president of the NACW at a meeting held in Baltimore. She began her tenure as president by reiterating her beliefs concerning the important role black women must play in the new century:

> No Negro woman can afford to be an indifferent spec-
> tator of the social, moral, religious, economic and uplift
> problems that are agitated around us. No Negro

woman can afford to be idle, but must take an active
personal interest in everything that concerns the welfare
of her home, her church, her community, her state, . . .
her religion.

In 1917 Mary put her private life aside and traveled to
Romagne, France, to serve as a Red Cross nurse to troops fighting
in the First World War. She traveled extensively throughout Europe
lecturing on the lives and problems of African Americans, especially women and children. She was later appointed to the League
of Nations Committee on International Relations.

When she returned home, President Warren Harding invited
her to travel across the country lecturing about the government's
food conservation program. Mary also used this opportunity to
campaign to secure voting rights for women. She knew that only
with the right to vote could any woman, no matter what race,
achieve any lasting improvements in their lives and those of their
families. In 1918, in addition to her position in the NACW, she
was elected vice president of the NAACP.

By 1918 Buffalo was experiencing an influx of African-
Americans from the southern states, drawn to the city by its
employment opportunities in the steel mills, the railroads, and
power plants. The older black residents found their position of
power challenged by the newcomers, many of whom were skilled
professionals. Some whites also felt threatened by the increase in
the black population, which presented competition for jobs and
businesses. Tensions increased between the races. The African-
American community felt increased pressure to develop a cohesive
network of support to counteract this tension.

Mary knew that such tension was detrimental to the black
cause, and she worked hard to lessen it. She kept in close contact
with editors of the local newspapers, encouraging them to tone

down sensationalism when reporting crimes committed by blacks. In 1922 she personally led a delegation of the NAACP to the editorial offices of the *Buffalo Times* to protest the publication of an advertisement recruiting members for the racist Ku Klux Klan.

Mary was in constant demand as a speaker. As president of the NACW, she knew she could not just concentrate on the Buffalo area and so continued to widen her area of concern throughout the country. She knew that conditions in the South were often much harsher for blacks, especially for their children. In South Carolina she discovered that boys as young as eight or nine were incarcerated with adult prisoners and forced to wear the black-and-white stripes of a convict for such petty offenses as stealing a watermelon. Children as young as five years of age were jailed for stealing food or a toy. Mary encouraged local NACW chapters to establish homes that would remove delinquent children from prisons and give them a chance to reform. She also petitioned the legislatures in the southern states to enact reforms in the laws governing the incarceration of children.

Indeed she campaigned for reforms in the treatment of all children, no matter what their race. In 1920 she attended the International Council of Women in Christiania, Norway, the first African-American delegate elected to attend. There she urged passage of a resolution that was named for her, the Talbert Resolution, which provided the right for all illegitimate children to bear their father's name and receive his financial support. Delegates returning to the United States were encouraged to lobby their legislators to enact the Talbert Resolution at home.

One of Mary's most ambitious projects as president of the NACW was the purchase and restoration of Anacostia, the home of the famous abolitionist Frederick Douglass, which was located in Washington, D.C. The NACW wished to preserve the home as a "monument to Douglass and black achievement" and also wished to use it as NACW headquarters because in Washington, D.C., they could manage the organization more efficiently and achieve greater visibility and accessibility to the government. By 1920 Mary was successful in raising the needed funds to purchase the home. The restoration was completed later and became a tribute to her memory.

In 1921 Mary became involved in a more pressing issue, the widespread problem of the lynching of blacks. Vigilante "citizen's committees," most prevalent throughout the southern states, were responsible for the hanging and shooting of dozens of unarmed blacks each year. The *New York World* newspaper reported in October 1922 that 264 African Americans were lynched in the United States during the five-year period of 1914–1918.

Mary was appalled by the lynchings. Using her position as vice president of the NAACP, she campaigned tirelessly for passage of a bill that was introduced to the House of Representatives by Missouri Congressman Leonidas Dyer that would make lynching a federal offense. Mary became the national director of the Anti-Lynching Crusade, raising over twelve thousand dollars through a nationwide lecture tour to support the Dyer antilynching bill.

When Congress failed to pass the bill, Mary refused to be discouraged. Instead she turned a setback into advantage. She urged the newly enfranchised women throughout the country to withhold their support of all those in Congress who had opposed the bill and to offer their support to those who did. Their efforts paid off. All the representatives who supported the bill were returned to Congress in the November 1922 elections. Thus Mary ably demonstrated to women the power that their newly won right to vote could wield and at the same time raised the consciousness of the entire country to the evils of lynching and the overt racism that it represented.

In 1922 the NAACP awarded Mary the coveted Spingarn Medal for her continued devotion to the cause of freedom and equality for blacks and all races. The Spingarn Medal, instituted in 1914 by former NAACP president J. E. Spingarn, is the NAACP's highest accolade, awarded for the "highest and noblest achievement by an African American." Mary was the first woman to receive the award.

In addition to public speaking, Mary was a frequent contributor to the black newspaper *The Crisis,* continuing to stress the importance of black women to their communities and to the nation as a whole.

But the constant traveling, speaking, writing, and battling for equal rights for her people began to take their toll. By 1922 Mary's health was failing. She died in Buffalo on October 15, 1923, and was buried at the Forest Lawn Cemetery. She was only fifty-seven years old. Her death was mourned by thousands. Newspaper headlines hailed her as "probably the most noted Negro woman in the world."

From the beginning of her public life, Mary was a passionate believer in the unique and powerful strength of women, especially women of her race. She continually fought the evils of persecution and inequality, deeply convinced that the impetus for change should and would come through the actions of women. To this end she campaigned for women's suffrage, believing it to be an essential component in the fight for equality for all races. She encouraged women to develop strong ties to their communities and to join both local and national organizations, such as the NACW and the NAACP. She campaigned tirelessly for the protection and promotion of black youth, especially through education, but she also sought to protect all human beings against human rights violations throughout the world. She wrote, "Clear and insistent is the call to the woman of my race today—the call to self-development and unselfish service. We cannot turn a deaf ear to the cries of the neglected little children, the untrained youth, the aged and the poor."

Throughout her life she drew all the ribbons of her experience and of her influence together to effect positive change for all races. But her first love was for her own race, for in the strength and honor of her people she never doubted. They loved and revered her, and she served them well.

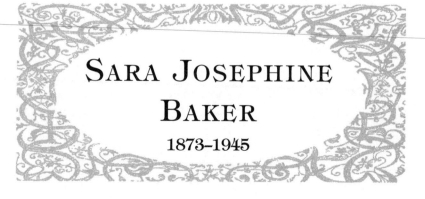

SARA JOSEPHINE BAKER
1873–1945

Champion of Health Care
for Children

*T*he corridor leading to the kitchen was dark, the house very still. Trailed by the nervous, young policeman, Josephine knocked tentatively at the kitchen door, not daring to imagine what she would find behind the carved oak panel. Suddenly the door swung open, and the young doctor was faced with the tall, angry form of the household cook wildly stabbing at her with a sharp carving fork. The fork missed Josephine's neck by just inches. Suddenly what had seemed like a routine call became for Sara Josephine Baker a fight for life.

The cook was a large woman—much larger than Josephine had imagined—tall and soundly built, with an unsmiling mouth set in a firm, angry line. She was dressed neatly in a shirtwaist dress covered with a clean apron, befitting her respected position as the family cook, charged with the task of nourishing the entire household.

But she was not nourishing this household. Far from it. Instead she was killing them or causing them to become very ill. From small children to elderly grandparents, from servants to

Sara Josephine Baker

master, no one was immune to the toxic germs of typhoid that she spread everywhere she went.

As an inspector for the New York City Health Department, young Doctor Baker had been assigned the task of obtaining certain specimens from the cook. Failing that, she was to bring the cook in to the hospital so the doctors could perform tests on her. But the cook, Mary Mallon, was frightened of these well-dressed strangers who were invading her kitchen. Mary firmly believed she had never had typhoid fever and was not a danger to anyone. As she waved her fork again, Josephine ducked and stepped back quickly into the corridor. Just as quickly the deadly cook and her fork disappeared.

For the next five hours, Josephine and the police searched frantically throughout that house and the house next door. Finally someone spotted a tiny bit of blue calico peeking from under a closet door. The police opened the door and there was Mary, who came out still fighting. Josephine again asked her to cooperate and again she refused. Finally the police carted Mary down to the ambulance by force. "I sat on her all the way to the hospital," Josephine later recalled. "It was like being in a cage with an angry lion."

Tests would prove that Mary Mallon did indeed carry the dreaded typhoid germs, and she would later be known as "Typhoid Mary." She infected many people and several died, even though she herself had never been very ill. Because she refused to stop cooking for a living, the Health Department was forced to keep her apart from society for the rest of her life. She never stopped blaming Sara Josephine Baker for the part she played in helping to make that happen.

In her medical career Josephine often encountered many like Mary Mallon—poor and desperate people who did not understand the benefits of preventive medicine. She often wondered why people had to become sick before visiting a doctor. Why not prevent illness in the first place by avoiding germs and following strict methods of personal hygiene? But preventive medicine was a new idea in 1907. Josephine had a long way to go before she would convince the public of its benefits.

Her experience with Mary Mallon taught Josephine an important lesson: about the power that the Board of Health had over people's lives. "There is very little that a Board of Health cannot do in the protection of the public health," she later realized. "Boards of Health have judicial, legislative, and executive powers, the only public agencies that combine all three powers." Later in her career as the head of New York City's Division of Child Hygiene, she would take advantage of such powers. The innovative practices she initiated would save the lives of thousands of babies and children and improve the lives of many others.

Born November 15, 1873, Sara Josephine Baker never dreamed she would become a doctor. But she did like to do things differently from other little girls. As the third daughter in a family of four children, she spent much of her childhood "trying to make it up to father for not being a boy," and so she became skilled at such tomboy activities as baseball and trout fishing. Even after the arrival of her brother Robert, she continued these activities and enjoyed them well into adulthood. Her family dropped the Sara part of her name when she was quite young and usually just called her Josephine, or Jo.

Josephine's father, Orlando Daniel Mosher Baker, was a prominent lawyer in Poughkeepsie, New York. Her mother, Jenny Brown, had been one of the first women to attend Vassar College. The family was a close-knit and happy group, taking full advantage of their proximity to the Hudson River to enjoy clambakes and boating parties in the summer and ice-skating and bobsledding in the winter. Despite the death of one of her sisters, Josephine's childhood was a happy one, spent in a round of dances and tennis matches and trips to the circus with her brother and his friends. As Josephine recalled in her autobiography, *Fighting for Life*, her childhood was "all precious . . . traditional small town stuff."

Josephine's conservative parents might have been surprised to learn that some of the professional success she later enjoyed was influenced at least in part by the teachings of an elderly Quaker aunt who was nearly one hundred years old when Josephine was a child. Aunt Abby lived an unorthodox life, sleeping all day and staying up all night. She was a favorite of the children of the family, whom she delighted by reading Bible stories and then deliberately and irreverently refuting any message those stories might convey. As Josephine tells it in her autobiography:

> She always read the story with much earnestness, and we hung on each word. Then, closing the book she would look at us benignly and say, "Now, children, that is a very silly story, and there is not a word of truth in it. Don't ever let anyone tell you that stories like that are true." I know it was the beginning of my desire to question the right and wrong of all accepted doctrines.

Josephine attended a small, undemanding school in Poughkeepsie run by the Misses Thomas, where there were no graded classes, no marks or reports, and no examinations. She planned to enter Vassar just as her mother had before her.

But when she was sixteen, those plans changed abruptly when both her father and brother died from typhoid fever. The residents of Poughkeepsie drew their drinking water directly from the Hudson River, and it was suspected that contaminated sewage from a hospital directly up the river had caused their deaths. Josephine and her mother and sister were devastated by their loss.

"We were an understanding trio," she later wrote, "my father, my brother and myself—and when they died so close together there seemed very little left to live for." Josephine's remaining sister was a semi-invalid and depended on their mother for her care. Feeling a deep sense of family responsibility, Josephine put her plans for attending Vassar aside and took on the daunting task of caring for the two of them and herself.

But what was she to do? There was very little money left after the funerals to pay for professional training. She was offered a partial scholarship to Vassar, but she did not look forward to years of study with no guarantee of financial return. Josephine shocked her entire family by announcing that she would become a doctor.

It was a strange choice of profession for a young woman in the late nineteenth century, and her reasoning in making this choice can only be speculated on. The deaths of her father and brother may have convinced her of the need for good medical care. Although there were very few women in the medical field at the time, she knew that as a doctor, she could always find work. But there were personal factors involved as well—her natural inclination to question accepted practice and her inordinate stubbornness in the face of disapproval. The response to her announcement from the rest of her family was overwhelmingly negative. They believed it to be an "unheard of, harebrained and unwomanly scheme." So she convinced her mother to give her $5,000 from her father's estate so she could study medicine "at all costs and in spite of everyone."

She was soon to learn, however, that her education at the Misses Thomas School had left her unprepared for such a challenge. It would take a solid year of cramming in such elementary subjects as chemistry and biology to bring her up to a level that met medical school requirements for acceptance. She finally entered the Women's Medical College of the New York Infirmary in 1894.

The school was founded in 1868 by the first woman physician, Dr. Elizabeth Blackwell, and her sister, Dr. Emily Blackwell, and was the only regular medical school available for women. Away at school for the first time, Josephine was lonely and worried she would not succeed. Her fellow students were older and seemed "seriously absorbed in their work." But gradually she became used to the intense program and began to make friends. After four years of hard work, Josephine graduated second in her class of eighteen students. She spent another year interning at the New England Hospital for Women and Children in Boston, finally emerging in 1899 to practice as a full-fledged doctor. The doubts of her skeptical Poughkeepsie relatives were irrevocably laid to rest.

She returned to New York fueled by optimism and opened a private practice with a friend on West 91st Street. Despite their high hopes, the two made almost no money for the first year. Not many people would seek the advice of a woman physician. It was only when a persistent life insurance salesman approached them to purchase policies that the two hit on a way to make money. They convinced the life insurance companies that prospective woman clients would much rather be examined by female doctors than by male doctors, so they were hired as insurance medical examiners. That job led Josephine to a job as a part-time medical inspector for the city of New York for the princely sum of thirty dollars a month, double her previous year's rate of income.

Her appointment to this position offered her firsthand experience with political corruption. When she was applying for the job, she had innocently asked a patient for a letter of recommendation. Later she learned she had been given the job not because of her qualifications, but because of her "connections." "That was my first lesson in the ways of the world of I'll-do-you-a-favor-sometime. It was also my launching in public health work," she later recalled.

The job required her to examine children in the public schools for disease and to send them home if there was any danger of contagion to the other children. But she was expected to cover three or four schools in one hour a day, clearly an impossible task. Many of her fellow inspectors never visited their schools at all and simply telephoned to check on the students every morning. Josephine routinely sent home any children that she found to have contagious skin or eye diseases, such as impetigo or trachoma. But her job was complicated by the local truant officers who sent the sick children back to school before they had sufficiently recovered.

In 1902 Josephine was offered a new job—that of seeking out sick babies on the west side of Manhattan. It paid the remarkable salary of one hundred dollars a month. The area—appropriately called Hell's Kitchen—was home to thousands of poor families. It was also home to poverty, filth, and disease, especially infant dysentery, a disease that causes severe dehydration and diarrhea in babies under one year of age, claiming the lives of an average of 1,500 babies each week. Josephine discovered that the mothers of these dying babies were distraught but fatalistic. Babies always died in the summer—there did not seem to be any way to change that. Funeral parades carrying tiny white caskets were a common everyday sight in Hell's Kitchen.

Josephine found the work to be exhausting and discouraging. Preventive medicine was unheard of, and mothers did not seek help in keeping their babies healthy. They only consulted a doctor when the children were sick. In her autobiography she recalled that for five long years she "climbed stair after stair, knocked on door after door, met drunk after drunk, filthy mother after filthy mother, and dying baby after dying baby."

In 1907 she was appointed assistant to the health inspector and had her fateful encounter with "Typhoid Mary" Mallon and her carving fork. Political problems, dysentery epidemics, and violent patients were certainly not what she had envisioned as her life's work when she decided to become a doctor!

One day she was called into the office of Dr. Walter Bensel, her immediate supervisor and the assistant sanitary superintendent. The city was interested in forming a new agency, the Division of Child Hygiene, and had decided to put her in charge of it. But there was a catch—before they allocated city funds for such a division, she would have to prove its value. With no money and only the assistance of thirty school nurses on vacation for the summer months, this would not be an easy task.

But Josephine's natural inclination to question accepted practice led her to formulate what seemed to be a daring plan. The summer season, when infants routinely died of dysentery, was just beginning. The registrar of records would send Josephine a daily list of the names and addresses of every baby born in Hell's Kitchen. When the baby and mother came home from the hospital, a nurse would visit them to discuss such beneficial practices as breast-feeding and outings in the fresh air. The nurse would also demonstrate the proper methods of bathing and dressing the babies. Could such a simple program of proper food, cleanliness, and fresh air prevent the traditional epidemic of newborn deaths in the summer months?

The results of the program were amazing! That summer there were 1,200 fewer deaths in that district than there had been the previous summer while the infant death rate for the rest of the city remained the same, even in the affluent areas. It was clear that Josephine's method of preventative medicine was a huge success. In August 1908 the Health Department officially created the Division of Child Hygiene, the first of its kind anywhere in the world. Josephine was appointed to head the new division, the first woman to hold an executive or administrative position in any health department. She was thirty-five years old.

The reality of being the first woman in such a position set in quickly—as soon as she was appointed her entire staff of six male doctors quit. It was nothing personal, they assured her, but they had never worked for a woman before and certainly had no intention of doing so now. Josephine remembered the scene in her autobiography:

> I needed those doctors to work with me. I asked them to sit down and talk it over. "See here," I said, "you are really crying before you are hurt. I quite realize that you may not like the idea of working under me as a woman. But isn't there another side of this question? I do not know whether I am going to like working with you. But if I am willing to take the responsibility of our success or failure, I think you might take a sporting chance with me."

The men agreed to give the arrangement a month's trial. In the end all six men stayed, and all eventually became devoted to her and to their work at the division.

Certainly there was plenty of work to go around. In future years Josephine would say that her new department had taken on the monumental responsibility of no less than "the superintendence of the child's well-being from before birth till he turned the corner into adulthood." It was to be her life's work.

In 1910 she turned her attention to the problem of untrained midwives delivering many of the babies in the tenements. Many poor women felt more comfortable with midwives than with doctors, especially because the use of midwives was something they had been accustomed to in their native countries. Medical doctors generally disapproved of the midwives, not only because they took away their patients, but also because the midwives' ignorance and lack of training often posed real health threats to the mothers and their babies. Josephine again challenged accepted practice—why not train the midwives to assist at births and require them to have a license? The school for midwives at Bellevue Hospital in New York City was begun, and all midwives in the city were required to obtain a license if they wanted to continue to practice.

Since milk was not yet pasteurized, Josephine urged the division to provide a system of milk stations that would provide families with clean, fresh milk at lower-than-market prices. She developed a unique formula from the milk that would be easy for babies to digest. On her visits to new babies, she often discovered that many mothers were routinely wrapping the babies so tightly that the babies suffocated. She developed a new style of clothing for babies that opened down the front for ease in dressing and changing. She also promoted the practice of putting one drop of silver nitrate solution in the eyes of newborn infants to prevent blindness, even developing an innovative packaging that controlled the dosage.

In many poor families both parents were forced to work outside the home, often leaving girls as young as nine or ten years old to care for babies and toddlers. Josephine's agency began a program called "The Little Mothers" to train young girls in all aspects of baby care. Not only did the girls learn to care competently for their own brothers and sisters, but they also encouraged young mothers in the tenements to come to the baby health stations where they would receive fresh milk and information on baby care. The Little Mothers program was later adopted in other cities and countries throughout the world.

The Division of Child Hygiene had achieved dazzling success in reducing the infant death rate in the tenements. But there was one place where babies still seemed to be dying for no reason, the city's foundling hospitals. Josephine was puzzled by the fact that although babies in these hospitals were given the best food and the most up-to-date health care, they often languished in their cribs and died. Convinced that all they needed was a sufficient dose of human warmth and love, she offered poor mothers a small monthly stipend to care for the babies in their own homes. The plan's unprecedented success attracted notice in the press, and in January 1913, the *New York Times* announced that the death rate for foster babies was one in three, as opposed to one in two for the babies left in the sterile hospital environment. Results for premature infants were even more remarkable: 50 percent of the boarded babies lived, while virtually all those hospitalized died.

Diseases of the tonsils and adenoids were very common in school-age children, and the city hospitals and clinics were swamped with children needing surgery. Josephine was horrified to discover that operations were sometimes actually performed in schools under unsanitary and frightening conditions. To counter-act this the division built small neighborhood clinics, which were limited exclusively to the performance of tonsillectomies and adenoidectomies. Children were brought in the day before their surgery. A caring staff member explained to them exactly what would happen during their surgery. Operations were performed in the morning, and the children were observed for a while and then sent home. This program brought a marked decrease in post-operative hemorrhage and infection. General hospitals throughout the city were eventually convinced of its wisdom and later adopted it themselves.

In 1918 Josephine faced real controversy when she insisted on keeping the New York City public schools open during the epidemic of influenza that was tearing through the city. She was convinced the children would be safer in school and less exposed to the disease than they would be out on the streets or in their homes all day long with other sick family members. But she faced the frightening possibility that if she were wrong, there would be many more sick children to worry about.

Again her innate common sense proved correct. When the epidemic was over, the statistics spoke for themselves: in children ages six to fifteen, there was no evidence of any epidemic that year, and school absences because of illness were actually lower than they had been the year before.

After twenty-five years of fighting for the health of the city's children, Sara Josephine Baker declared she would retire when every state provided a Department of Child Hygiene, and in 1923 she made good on her promise. Her mother died in 1924, and her remaining sister died soon after. She closed the family home in Poughkeepsie and moved to a farm in New Jersey that she shared with some friends.

But she certainly did not retire from public life. In 1935 she accepted the presidency of the American Medical Women's Association. She continued to lecture on child hygiene at New York and Columbia Universities. In later years she wrote over two hundred articles for popular and professional journals, five books on child health and welfare, and her autobiography, *Fighting for Life*. She died of cancer in New York City in 1945 at the age of seventy-five.

Like many women of her era who had chosen traditionally male professions, Josephine often faced disapproval and ostracism. She was no stranger to failure—some of what she considered her best ideas met with defeat. She was unsuccessful in convincing school officials of the benefits of well-ventilated classrooms and was always dismayed when classroom windows and doors stayed firmly shut because school officials were concerned with noise and heating bills. Her attempts to promote preventive dentistry met with failure because many of the techniques of cavity prevention had simply not been discovered yet.

But she also met with unprecedented success. When she began her public health career in 1908, the infant mortality rate in New York City was 144 per 1,000 live births. When she retired in 1923, it was 66, one of the lowest of any of the major cities in the United States or Europe. She also achieved many impressive "firsts" as a woman: the first to head a municipal health department, the first to represent the United States at the League of Nations, and in 1917 the first to obtain a doctoral degree in public health. Through all of her programs, experiments, and initiatives, she held true to her belief that the path to success depended on preventing problems before they started, on "questioning the unquestionable," and on challenging the prevalent way of thinking. Aunt Abby's lesson was not forgotten.

Josephine spent her life trying to secure good health care for all women and children, but she never forgot the thrill of saving a single life, the "joy she saw in a mother's eyes when her baby was assured of health." Although her life had been a difficult struggle, she said in her autobiography, "I would not have any of it different in any way. It was a magnificent opportunity, a great and heart-warming experience, a happy road to follow. A glorious, an exhilarating and an altogether satisfactory life."

GERTRUDE VANDERBILT WHITNEY

1875–1942

Patron of American Art

$\mathcal{T}$he heiress Gertrude Vanderbilt Whitney was shocked. Her assistant, Juliana Force, was stunned. They could scarcely believe the reaction to their most generous offer. They had spent years amassing over six hundred works of contemporary American art—probably the largest collection of its kind anywhere—but they were running out of storage and exhibiting room in their gallery on 8th Street in Greenwich Village. And so in what they felt was an act of immense generosity, they offered the entire collection as a gift to the newly opened Metropolitan Museum of Art on Fifth Avenue in New York City. Gertrude was even prepared to spend several million dollars to fund the construction of a wing to house the gift.

Such an offer made eminent sense. In addition to commanding a fortune, Gertrude was herself a sculptor of some renown. Her family was already closely associated with the Metropolitan Museum; her father, Cornelius Vanderbilt II, had served as chairman of the executive committee and was a frequent and generous donor of both money and works of art.

Gertrude Vanderbilt Whitney

But much to their bewilderment, their offer was flatly refused. The director of the Metropolitan Museum, Dr. Edward Robinson, did not feel the need to house or exhibit a collection of strictly American art because frankly he saw no value in it. After the meeting with Robinson, Gertrude, Juliana, and journalist Forbes Watson lingered around the lunch table of a nearby restaurant debating what to do next, and as the afternoon waned, and the sun shifted toward the west, they came to a momentous decision. If the Metropolitan did not want their collection, they would open a museum of their own that would exhibit only the art of their countrymen. It would be called, aptly, the Whitney Museum of American Art.

In 1929 this was an outrageous idea. American art and artists commanded little respect in the early part of the twentieth century. Those who could afford to invest in art preferred classical European art, such as that of Paul Cézanne, Paul Gauguin, and Vincent Van Gogh. Wealthy art patrons were averse to spending money on the works of such American artists as John Sloan or George Luks. But Gertrude was fully committed to the ideal that "the public should know the art of its people." With her support the Whitney Museum of American Art would grow to be the definitive center of the art of the American people.

Certainly Gertrude could afford to support such an endeavor. She was born on January 9, 1875, into the richest family in America and was raised in an atmosphere of immense wealth and privilege. She lived much of her life in the rarefied air of a French-style chateau on Fifth Avenue in New York City that boasted 137 rooms. Pampered by servants and governesses, she was privately educated, had an elaborate wardrobe even as a child, and spent summers either abroad or at the family summer "cottage" in Newport, Rhode Island.

Gertrude's great-grandfather was Cornelius Vanderbilt, who rose from the obscurity of a poor Dutch family to become the richest man in America. In 1810, at the age of sixteen, he borrowed a hundred dollars from his mother and began his own ferry business between Staten Island and New York City. When he died in 1877 at the age of eighty-three, he was worth over $100 million, a fortune amassed by maintaining ruthless control of shipping and railroad lines in New York. Most of this fortune went to his son William, Gertrude's grandfather, who doubled the family's worth before his death and passed on a substantial amount of it to his son Cornelius II, Gertrude's father. At the time of her birth, Gertrude's father, like his grandfather before him, was believed to be the richest man in the world.

Yet superimposed on this life of luxury and privilege was an atmosphere of oppression and emptiness that Gertrude would work her entire life to overcome. In keeping with her station in society, her upbringing was severe. One of seven children of Alice Gwynne and Cornelius Vanderbilt II, her personal conduct was the subject of constant scrutiny by her parents and governesses. Strict rules were imposed on all manner of dress, speech, and interaction with others. A proper young lady did not show anger, did not complain, and did not entertain outbursts of any kind, including those of affection. Proper and elaborate dress was the norm, and she could never forget that her family was always in the public eye. Any breach of this code of conduct could be grounds for social disgrace for the entire family. Despite her sensitive nature, Gertrude learned at an early age to mask her emotions and to offer an aloof and reserved countenance to the world, all the while worrying over the knowledge that "all the money in the world cannot buy . . . a loving heart or a true friend."

From the age of ten, she was a prolific diarist, writing at length both about the social occasions in her life and her deepest longings. Her diaries were replete with notes about table settings, guest lists of different social functions, and descriptions of what everyone wore. But she also wrote copious letters to family members filled with personal feelings—letters that were never mailed because she simply could not speak freely to them of her intimate thoughts and desires.

At the age of fourteen, she entered the Brearley School, a private school for girls in New York City, and an excellent choice for the shy, young girl. At a time when it was thought girls needed only to know enough about the arts and sciences to be a gracious wife and mother, the Brearley School imposed on its students an ambitious curriculum of language, mathematics, history, science, and Latin. Gertrude thrived under such tutelage, showing talent for watercolor and writing. She even hoped to continue her education after graduating in 1894. But her parents and society had different plans for her. She came out as a debutante in the 1894–95 social season, and in 1896 she was married to Harry Payne Whitney, a young man within her social circle whose family fortune—while not approaching the Vanderbilts'—was substantial.

Gertrude loved Harry. Throughout her childhood she had never been quite sure whether anyone would love her for herself, not her fortune. She worried if there would ever be a time "that the money could make no difference." At least married to the dashing and wealthy Harry Payne Whitney, she would not have such worries, she thought. The young couple honeymooned in Japan and returned home to take up residence in a house just down the block from her parents.

But if Gertrude thought that marriage would allow her a breath of freedom from social strictures, she was sadly mistaken. The life of a wealthy, young, married woman in 1896 was a dizzying round of dinners, balls, and visiting, and for Gertrude it included ceaseless travel between her and Harry's house on Fifth Avenue; their estate in Old Westbury, Long Island; and their "cottage" in Newport, Rhode Island. Within the next three years, she gave birth to two children, and her family and social obligations left her little time to follow any artistic instincts she might have had.

As a husband Harry Payne Whitney soon proved a disappointment. Harry was good-looking and charming but without a single inclination toward work of any kind. He dabbled in law and politics but soon tired of such pursuits. Instead he devoted himself to playing at polo, golf, and racing. There were rumors of infidelities. Gertrude's diary tells of her unhappiness, of looking "into a future that held neither pleasure nor satisfaction," and the frustration of finding a real focus for her energies.

She had always been a prolific writer, penning short stories, several novels, and writing religiously in her diary. But Gertrude was fearful that her writing would expose the emptiness of her life and embarrass her family. She turned to sculpture, first working on a small scale and then moving up to larger pieces.

Sculpture was freeing for Gertrude and marked a tremendously daring departure from the staunchly conservative environment in which she had grown up. Sculpture allowed her—indeed required her—to become intimately familiar with the human anatomy. She used male nudes as models, much to the consternation of her mother. Alice Vanderbilt was shocked by Gertrude's sculptures, and after seeing her work on a nude statue once implored her, "Do give him a scarf . . . the fig leaf is so little!"

Gertrude began studying with Hendrik Christian Andersen and later with Charles Chester French. She traveled to Paris where she studied under Andrew O'Conner and received criticism from August Rodin. Back home she rented a studio on West 57th Street and built another on her estate in Newport. Charles Chester French had a studio in Greenwich Village in a bohemian neighborhood populated by other artists and sculptors, and it was there that Gertrude finally began to feel comfortable with herself as an artist.

A third child was born to Gertrude and Harry in 1903, but it was not an easy pregnancy, and Gertrude was not as delighted with this child as she had been with the first two. She began to devote more time to her art, even though neither her husband nor her mother ever took it very seriously. Her contact with other artists showed her how difficult it was to succeed as an artist without money or patronage. It was then that she finally began to appreciate her famous name and fortune and realize that she could use them both to further her own projects and help other artists as well. In 1907 she opened a studio on MacDougal Street in Greenwich Village and offered American artists not only gallery space to exhibit their work, but housing and stipends to support them in their efforts as well.

The first decade of the new century saw the emergence of the dynamic and daring movement of realism: art that portrayed real-life themes instead of the stylized and romantic approach of the "old masters." Paintings such as John Sloan's *McSorley's Bar* and George Luks's *Hester Street* explored an interest in common street themes that was new to the art world. Gertrude was actively working to support such struggling artists and purchase intriguing new works of American art, while working at and promoting her own career as a sculptor. But she needed someone to help her coordinate those efforts and free her for her own work.

Juliana Reiser Force came into Gertrude's life in 1907 when Juliana was secretary to Gertrude's sister-in-law, Helen Hay Whitney. Juliana had her own business. She supported herself as a secretary and typist at a time when such an independent professional lifestyle was unthinkable for most young women. She was well acquainted with the manners and customs of Gertrude's world, worked like a dervish, and was trustworthy and discreet, qualities Gertrude and other members of her closed society particularly appreciated. And best of all, she was a great fan of American art and artists.

Gertrude admired her, and she and Juliana complemented each other beautifully. Juliana was vivacious and outspoken and determined to rise above her modest upbringing in Hoboken, New Jersey. Gertrude was shy and constricted by her social milieu, but she could offer Juliana entrée into a world that she would have otherwise never known—a world of wealth, privilege, and excitement. Juliana in turn offered Gertrude a chance to achieve her own personal goals. They began working together in 1907 and would form a cohesive and successful team for the rest of Gertrude's life.

In 1908 Gertrude won her first art prize for a collaboration with architect Grosvenor Atterbury and mural painter Hugo Ballin on a design for an outdoor swimming pool and pavilion. Gertrude's contribution was a statue of Pan arising from a fountain. The design won an award from the Architectural League, but the group came under criticism because Mr. Atterbury was actually chairman of the prize committee. Gertrude refused the prize money. For several years afterward she exhibited her work under an assumed name, fearing her work was not being judged objectively because of her name and family connections.

In 1913 she commissioned the architectural firm of Delano and Aldrich to build her another studio at the family's Old Westbury estate on Long Island. There she spent long hours working on her sculpture, usually solid and muscular figures endowed with a strong, physical force. In 1912 she was commissioned to create a terra-cotta Aztec fountain for the patio of the Pan American Building in Washington, D.C., and in 1914 she created a soaring figure for the Titanic Memorial in Potomac Park.

Gertrude and Harry were living increasingly separate lives, hers devoted to art, his to pleasure. But private concerns were thrust aside in 1914 with the outbreak of World War I in Europe. Gertrude was appalled by the reality that her beloved France might suffer in the war and decided to do something positive besides simply donate money. She appealed to Harry to help her, but he was unsympathetic, so she used her own money (an estimated one million dollars) to finance a shipment of doctors, nurses, and medical supplies to Juilly. She traveled there in November 1914 on the *Lusitania* and set up a 225-bed hospital very near the frontlines. At home Juliana arranged an art exhibit and sale at the gallery on 8th Street to raise funds for war relief. "If this experience has done nothing else," Gertrude wrote in her diary, "it has made me see more clearly the line of usefulness in life and cast behind me more ruthlessly these people who will acknowledge no duties or responsibilities."

Gertrude's experiences in World War I did more than emphasize her differences with her husband. Her days at the front brought home to her in graphic detail the horrors of war: soldiers suffering, nurses straining to save lives, piled bodies awaiting burial. Gertrude would never have seen such things if she had stayed home in the safety and comfort of her secure world. These experiences were later reflected in her art, which became more naturalistic and impressionistic, a departure from the stylized, large monuments of her past. She returned home to create many moving sculptures of soldiers—sculptures that offered her personal expression of the horrors of war.

In 1918, continuing her personal drive to help other artists, she opened the Whitney Studio Club, an outgrowth of the old Whitney Studio in Greenwich Village, with Juliana Force as director. For a modest five-dollar annual dues, the club offered young artists not only a gallery to create and exhibit their work, but a comfortable place to socialize with other artists. The membership roster would eventually grow to include over four hundred names, including such charter members as Edward Hopper, Rockwell Kent, and John Dos Passos, who wrote as well as painted. With Juliana's help, Gertrude continued to purchase the works of young artists, amassing a collection of hundreds of sculptures and paintings that would later be refused by the Metropolitan Museum of Art and would form the core collection of the Whitney Museum of American Art when it opened in 1931.

In 1924 Gertrude returned to France to create the St. Nazaire Monument, which was erected on a rocky prominence where the first American troops had landed during the war. That same year the Buffalo Bill Historical Center in Wyoming commissioned a statue of Buffalo Bill—a thirteen-foot-tall rearing horse and rider that perfectly captured the subject's adventurous spirit. In 1929 she was commissioned to create a representation of Columbus. Her work soon towered 114 feet over the port of Palos in Spain.

Gertrude's reputation as a respected sculptor in her own right was firmly established, but never without personal struggle. As a child she was never quite sure if her friends only loved her because her name was Vanderbilt. As an artist she continually worried that her art would not be taken seriously for the same reason.

Her personal life continued to be tumultuous. Her children grew up, married, and divorced. Her husband continued to lead his own life, overseeing various business interests while building a successful horse-racing stable and breeding farm. Harry excelled at polo and served as captain of the American team that won the International Cup three times. Their marriage became an increasingly impersonal arrangement, but one that neither of them chose to terminate. There was a special bond between them that their differences never severed.

The Metropolitan Museum of Art refused Gertrude's offer of her American art collection just weeks before the momentous

1929 stock market crash that would plunge the country into one of the deepest financial depressions it had ever known. Despite an obvious reduction in their personal fortunes, Harry did not waver in his support for the new Whitney Museum of American Art and encouraged Gertrude to go ahead with her plans. But Harry never lived to see the museum open. He died on October 26, 1930, from pneumonia, leaving a fortune of about sixty million dollars to his wife and children and various charities.

The opening of the Whitney Museum on November 18, 1931, was a bittersweet experience for Gertrude without Harry to share it with her, but it was enthusiastically received by the public, who streamed through its rooms. The *New York Times* called the exhibition "impressive":

> The Whitney Museum wisely presents the best our artists can produce and invites the public to arrive at its own conclusions. . . . So many individual styles and tendencies are revealed, frequently at their best, that the spectacle is full of variety. It sparkles and vibrates with life. Every wall is alive with invitations that solicit pause and lead the eye on to fresh adventures.

With the museum off to a promising start, Gertrude's life resumed its comfortable blend of family and social duties, combined with her work at the museum and on her own sculptures. The year 1934 saw the end of a bitter and protracted court battle between Gertrude and her sister-in-law, Gloria Morgan Vanderbilt, for custody of Gloria Vanderbilt, the daughter of Gertrude's deceased brother Reggie Vanderbilt. The case had been publicized in the newspaper for months; its final disposition gave Gertrude custody of the child with visits from her mother, but left Gertrude exhausted and discouraged.

She continued to work with Juliana Force, managing and choosing the work of such artists as John Steuart Curry, John LaFarge, and Thomas Hart Benton for the Whitney, and personally funding virtually all the works collected by the museum. Her last major sculpting commission was the *Spirit of Flight*, designed for the New York World's Fair of 1939–40. As her strength and health failed, she reluctantly abandoned her sculpting and returned to writing to express herself. After a brief illness, she died on April 18, 1942.

Gertrude Vanderbilt Whitney was an anomaly in the story of privilege and wealth in the early years of the twentieth century. The life she was born into predicted a destiny for her exactly like others of her class, that of a primarily useless but pleasant dilettante concerned mostly with rounds of social engagements and frivolities.

But Gertrude was different. She deplored the banality of the lives of many of her peers and sought instead a life of useful labor. She fought to overcome the prejudice of her own class—including that of her own family and friends—and pursued her talent as a sculptor when such a career and the art it produced was considered unseemly at best and scandalous at worst. At times it seemed as if her wealth was a detriment rather than a benefit. But she rose above such concerns, and in the end her work spoke for her talent more eloquently than any glowing review could.

But her own work comes a close second to what many consider to be her greatest achievement, her unswerving belief in and devotion to the work of American artists. Her consistent and unflinchingly generous support of American art forced the art world to finally take it seriously. In 1963 the Whitney Museum moved to Madison Avenue and continues to this day Gertrude's legacy of nurturing, exhibiting, and honoring the finest in American art.

Despite her talent Gertrude had remained modest about her own achievements, so when the Whitney held a memorial exhibit of Gertrude's works after her death, it marked the first time so many of her works were exhibited in one place. In the catalogue that accompanied the memorial exhibition, her good friend Juliana Force wrote:

> Though she is no longer with us, her ideals remain to participate in our cultural life, to give form and coherence to the art of our time and country and to help us shape the world that is to come. . . . It is appropriate that this museum which is a symbol of her faith in the future should now contain this exhibition of her sculpture. Together they form a fitting memorial to the creative achievements of a gifted artist and of a wise and generous woman.

Dorothy Day
1897–1980

Founder of the Catholic
Worker Movement

The flames of the votive candles flickered feebly in the waning hours of the December afternoon. The young woman kneeling at the shrine shivered a bit and clutched at her coat. The night was cold; the day had been even colder, as if reflecting sharply her own personal anguish.

She was no newcomer to anguish; indeed it had been a close companion for much of her life. But tonight was different. She had come to the shrine at the Catholic University in Washington, D.C., on the feast of the Immaculate Conception, after a day of political unrest in the nation's capitol. It was a day of marches and speeches and bands of ragged, hungry demonstrators waving flags for justice and demanding work and food. It was 1932, the middle of the Great Depression. But her prayers were not for those demonstrators on their hunger march, as worthy as their needs might be. Instead her prayers were unashamedly for herself.

Her life seemed suddenly without meaning. The religion she had sacrificed to join seemed distant. She prayed for a way to use her talents to help her fellow man—the poor, the destitute, the workers of the world—and for a way to ease her own loneliness. The next day she returned home to her apartment in New York City, to her daughter and her well-ordered existence, and met a man who would change her life forever.

Dorothy Day would join her talents and energies with those of Peter Maurin to found the Catholic Worker Movement. Together they would write the *Catholic Worker* newspaper, feed the poor, comfort the sick and needy, take pacifists' stand against war and the use of weapons, and try to fulfill the teachings of Jesus Christ and the Catholic Church. It would not be an easy life. It would be filled with hard work and riddled with controversy, but it would bring her much joy and ultimately a consideration for nothing less than sainthood by the Roman Catholic Church.

Dorothy Day was born November 8, 1897, in Brooklyn, New York. Hers was a restless childhood that stretched from New York City to San Francisco and back east to the poverty-stained streets of Chicago and New York. Her father, John Day, was of Scotch-Irish heritage, from a patriotic Tennessee family that had fought for the Confederacy during the Civil War. Her mother was born Grace Satterlee and was of English ancestry. The Satterlee family lived in Marlboro, New York, and had fought the Civil War on the side of the Union.

Dorothy's father was a sportswriter; her mother was a home-maker who cared for the family of three boys and two girls. Dorothy was the third child and oldest daughter. When Dorothy was six years old, her father moved the family from New York to Oakland, California.

Although she attended a Methodist Sunday school, her family was not particularly religious. Once Dorothy questioned her mother as to why they did not "pray and sing hymns." But the children were taught simple prayers and were imbued at an early age with a sense of right and wrong, of good and evil. Dorothy attended church with a neighbor, becoming "disgustingly, proudly pious," while at the same time deeply afraid of God, death, and eternity.

The family's quiet life was shattered on April 18, 1906, by the rumbling of an earthquake that shook San Francisco, gorging huge chasms in the earth and setting fires everywhere. Although the family itself was intact, their home was a shambles of broken dishes and fallen chimneys. Oakland escaped the fires, but the flames from the city could be seen from across the bay, and refugees flooded over by ferry and boat. Dorothy helped her mother and their neighbors distribute clothing to the homeless; she remembered later that "every stitch of available clothing was given away."

The newspaper where John Day worked suffered damage by fire and could no longer publish. Although the Red Cross offered aid to families affected by the earthquake, John Day was too proud to accept such aid for his family. Instead he sold most of the household furnishings and moved the family to Chicago, where he took a job as sports editor for a Chicago paper, *The Inter Ocean.*

Because her father worked at night, Dorothy and her siblings were discouraged from having friends in during the day while he slept. They sought pleasure in reading and taking long walks through the city, pushing baby brother John in his carriage. Dorothy read Dickens, Jack London, and Upton Sinclair's *The Jungle.* But her childhood was laced with periods of depression, when a "heavy and abiding sense of loneliness and sadness" overcame her. Such moods were to plague her throughout her life.

At age sixteen Dorothy won a scholarship to the University of Illinois. Here she joined the Socialist Party and became increasingly aware of the gap between the rich and the poor. She herself had little money and cared for children to pay for her board and books. And although as a child she had experienced an obsessive thrill with religion, as a young women she turned against it, concurring with the Marxist belief that religion was an "opiate of the masses," designed to keep them poor and oppressed. She attended the university but disdained formal study, frequently missing classes. Finally when she was eighteen, she left the university altogether to accompany her family when they moved back to New York.

In New York, Dorothy worked as a reporter for the Socialist newspaper *The Call.* She walked picket lines, witnessed strikes in garment factories, and wrote about the plight of the destitute in the city's tenements. She found the poverty of New York even worse than that of Chicago and described it vividly in her autobiography, *The Long Loneliness:*

> The poverty of New York was appallingly different from that of Chicago. The sight of homeless and workless men sleeping in doorways appalled me. . . . The smell from the tenements, coming up from base-ments and dank halls horrified me. . . . It is a smell like no other in the world, one never can become accus-tomed to it. . . . It is not the smell of life but the smell of the grave.

Yet, it was in those slums that she lived, renting a cheap apartment on Cherry Street in lower Manhattan. Her colleagues from *The Call* were self-proclaimed socialists, labor organizers, and "free thinkers." At times her burgeoning idealism brought her more trouble than she had bargained for. When she traveled to Washington to protest the treatment of imprisoned suffragists, she ended up being arrested herself, sentenced to spend thirty days in jail, then joining her comrades in a hunger strike. The experience was a sobering one. One of the members of her group, a teacher, was chained to the bars of the cell. Another was force-fed. They lived in squalid conditions, in cold, dank cells. She began for the first time to question the efficacy of such movements, to wonder if their efforts might not be in vain.

The next few years saw her lead a bohemian lifestyle that she later described as "dissolute, wasted, full of sensuality." She had relationships with several men, became pregnant by one, and had an abortion when he deserted her. She married and divorced soon after. She signed up for a year of nurse's training but left when the work became impossibly hard. She worked on a novel. Charles Shipman described her during that time in his book *It Had to Be Revolution* as "raw-boned, square-jawed, compelling sexy, game for anything unrespectable, the more outrageous the better."

But amazingly, at the same time, Catholicism was slowly making an impact on her life, weaving its way into her daily routine, tantalizing her with its promises of forgiveness and eternal life. She began to attend Mass with her roommates and to pay late-night visits to St. Joseph's Catholic Church on Sixth Avenue.

And then Dorothy fell in love.

She was living on Staten Island in a small bungalow she had purchased with the proceeds she'd received from selling the movie rights to her novel, *The Eleventh Virgin*. The $5,000 was a fortune, a blessing that finally allowed her to return to writing full time. She woke to the sounds of the surf, took long walks on the beach, and cultivated friendships with her bohemian neighbors. Her lover, Forster Battingham, was not part of the literary or radical groups she had previously been associated with. Perhaps that was part of his charm for her. She described him in her autobiography:

> The man I loved, with whom I entered a common-law marriage was an anarchist, an Englishman by descent, and a biologist. His mother and father had both come

from England, and he and his seven sisters were born in
Asheville, North Carolina. . . . We fished together, we
walked every day for miles, we studied together, and a
whole new world opened up for me.

Quite suddenly Dorothy was happy. She entered into a halcyon
time with her lover, and when she discovered she was pregnant, it
only added to her happiness. Throughout her pregnancy prayer
became an increasingly important part of her life. She began
attending Mass regularly on Sunday mornings, and long before the
baby was born, she decided she would have it baptized in the
Catholic Church.

But Forster disapproved of religion. Dorothy knew that if
she became a Catholic, she could no longer sustain her common-
law relationship with him. They quarreled, and a rift began
between them that would widen beyond the ability of either of
them to repair.

Their daughter was born on March 3, 1927, and was named
Tamar Theresa. Dorothy's joy at the birth of her daughter knew
no bounds. The day after Tamar's birth she wrote an article for the
New Masses, wanting to share that joy with the world. But with that
joy came fear and sorrow. She wanted desperately to have the baby
baptized in the Catholic Church. "I knew I was not going to have
her floundering through many years as I had done, doubting and
hesitating, undisciplined and amoral." But in embracing Catholicism she knew she would lose Forster and the quiet joy they
shared.

Dorothy made her difficult choice. She and her daughter
were baptized soon afterward, and they began their life together
alone. They moved into the apartment of Dorothy's brother and

Dorothy Day in the 1920s

his wife. The next five years were spent working and traveling. She supported herself and her daughter through a series of writing jobs, including a screenwriter's job in California. It was while she was on assignment for a Catholic newspaper, the *Commonweal*, that she spent that cold night at the shrine of the Immaculate Conception in Washington, D.C., praying for guidance. And it was the next day that she met Peter Maurin, and her new life began.

Peter Maurin burst into Dorothy Day's life with an intensity that both startled and intrigued her. George Schuster, editor of the *Commonweal*, had given him Dorothy's address, and when she came home to New York from Washington, he was waiting for her in the apartment she shared with her brother's family. Although he had never met Dorothy, he was convinced that as a journalist she could help him write a newspaper that would enable him to share his radical ideas with others, ideas that he was convinced would ultimately change the world for the better.

Peter was a stocky, rugged-looking man who wore borrowed clothes and spoke with a heavy foreign accent. He had been born in France into a devout family of twenty-three children. As a young man he had studied with the Christian Brothers, had learned about the lives of the saints, and had become steeped in Benedictine spirituality. He later moved to Canada. When he came to New York to meet Dorothy, he was working without pay at a summer camp for children in upstate New York.

But it was not his appearance, nor his heritage that intrigued Dorothy Day. It was his tremendous ambition to found nothing less than a new world order, a "new society in the shell of the old." His ideal was that of "personalism," a concept that tries to bridge the gap between life and faith. Personalists seek to cultivate a disposition to grow in active love toward all creation, thus "creating a society where it is easier for men to be good."

Dorothy explained in her autobiography:

Peter rejoiced to see men do great things and dream
great dreams. He wanted them to stretch their arms out
to their brothers, because he knew that the surest way to
find God . . . was through one's brothers. He wanted
them to be able to produce what was needed in the way
of homes, food, clothing, so that there was enough of
these necessities for everyone—a synthesis of "cult,
culture and cultivation"—the three necessary aspects of
an integrated life.

Peter believed that men must accept the goodness of God in
others, even if they could not see it. He espoused poverty because
it freed him from the need to compete for material goods. He
envisioned "houses of hospitality" where the poor would be
welcomed, fed, and sheltered. He dreamed of farm colonies where
the unemployed would find work growing their own food. But
while he talked incessantly, "his whole body compelling your
attention," he was not arrogant and was careful of others' feelings
and ideas.

Peter followed Dorothy around for months, lecturing,
recommending reading materials, talking to her and at her non-
stop. Most of the time she listened. Sometimes she tired of his
lecturing and avoided him, not sure if she even believed in his
radical ideas. But in the end she knew that his was the combina-
tion of work and faith for which she had been searching. It seemed
that Dorothy Day and Peter Maurin were quite simply the answer
to each other's most heartfelt prayers.

He wanted to feed the soul. Dorothy worried about the body.
He wanted to publish a paper teaching and sharing his beliefs.
Dorothy asked where the money would come from. "Just read the

lives of the saints," Peter exhorted her. "In the history of the saints, capital was raised by prayer. God sends you what you need when you need it."

In the end he won her over. Dorothy and Peter wrote the *Catholic Worker* on her kitchen table with the help of her brother and his wife. They used the rent money to print the first issue of 2,500 copies, published by the Paulist Press for fifty-seven dollars. On May 1, 1933, this first issue was sold on the streets of New York City for one cent per copy, a sum they chose because they felt it was one almost anyone could afford.

The first issue was filled with articles about the cares of the working man: racial injustice and unemployment. Peter Maurin was at first upset by the tone of the paper. He wanted a voice for his writings and ideas exclusively. "Everybody's newspaper is nobody's paper," he lamented. But Dorothy knew the paper should be more than that. It should reflect the lives of its namesakes, the workers themselves.

The *Catholic Worker* was an instant success. Its articles struck a common chord in readers who were struggling through the Great Depression, and circulation rose steadily. By the end of 1933, it reached 100,000 people each month, and by the end of 1936, circulation was 150,000 copies a month. Often it was given away for free. Dorothy wrote a column for every issue, which she first called "Day by Day" (sometimes "Day after Day") and later changed to "On Pilgrimage."

The paper spurred what became known as the Catholic Worker movement. Catholic Workers opened their first Hospitality House, a forerunner of today's homeless shelters/soup kitchens, downstairs from Dorothy's apartment. Hundreds of men and women lined up every day for food. Other houses soon followed. Volunteers came to help write the paper and work in the houses. Many of those volunteers went on to open other Hospitality

Houses throughout the nation. Catholic Workers next began farm communities to serve the needy, from hungry migrant workers to unwed mothers who had nowhere else to go. Volunteers of all ages were attracted to these communities, to this cause that seemed to promise a sense of community. Peter Maurin's dream of offering shelter and food to the poor and homeless was becoming a reality.

Although the *Catholic Worker* published many articles about labor problems, its founders continually emphasized that its focus was on sharing the social teachings of Christ with the "men in the street," not inciting them to riot or strike. Indeed, Dorothy and Peter faced opposition, not over accusations that they incited violence, but over their intense belief in pacifism.

Dorothy believed firmly in the teachings of Jesus put forth in the Sermon on the Mount, in which he exhorted his followers to "be righteous, be meek, be pure of heart, be a peacemaker, be merciful. Blessed are the peacemakers, for they shall be called sons of God." When the Spanish Civil War began in July 1936, many American Catholics supported Francisco Franco, believing that the opposing Loyalist government was Communist dominated. The *Catholic Worker* announced it was pacifist and refused to take sides, a position that cost it many subscriptions and attracted much criticism.

The criticism intensified when the United States entered World War II in December 1941. Dorothy and her colleagues continued their pacifist stand, opposing the draft and encouraging young men to declare themselves as conscientious objectors. But dissention was growing, even within the movement itself. Few could understand the ideals of pacifism in the face of Hitler and the horrors of the Nazi domination of Europe.

But Dorothy would not compromise her ideals. In the January 1942 issue of the *Catholic Worker,* she wrote in her column, "We will print the words of Christ who is always with us: 'Love

MARQUETTE UNIVERSITY

Dorothy Day in 1938

your enemies, do good to those who hate you and pray for those who persecute and calumniate you.' We are at war . . . with Japan, Germany and Italy. But we can still repeat Christ's words each day, holding them close in our hearts."

World War II became a pivotal point of change for Dorothy Day and the Catholic Worker movement. There were more jobs supporting the war effort and thus fewer people on the bread lines, fewer in need of hospitality houses. By the end of the war, there were only ten houses still in operation. Many of the idealistic young people who had flocked to the movement were either at camps for conscientious objectors or in military service. Dorothy's daughter Tamar was on her own, happily married, and beginning a family.

Peter Maurin suffered what was thought to be a stroke. His mind failing, he spent his days sitting quietly in the sun, no longer lecturing or teaching. His death in May 1949 was a hard blow for Dorothy, bringing her an immense sense of loss. He had been a moving force in her life and the life of the movement for ten years. She had always found in his spirit a source of strength and inspiration. "Peter was an apostle to this world," she said in her autobiography. "He loved people and saw in them what God meant them to be, as he saw the world as God meant it to be, and loved it."

By the 1950s there were those proclaiming that the Catholic Worker movement had "seen its day," that the need for it was diminished. Dorothy and the movement again came under fire for her stand against atomic weapons and for what seemed to be a tolerance of Communism. The country was experiencing an intense anti-Communist era. Dorothy sometimes met with the Communist groups and tried to clarify her relationship with them by explaining that she attended these meetings to "bring them the message of the spirit," but there were many who did not believe her and suspected her of being a Communist herself.

Although discouraged by these attacks, she continued her work—traveling for months at a time, visiting the hospitality houses and farm communities, and offering encouragement, support, and inspiration for continuation of the work she and Peter had begun. She usually traveled by bus and stayed in the hospitality houses themselves, and she always lived her own life simply, espousing poverty and religious thought. She attended Mass daily, read the lives of the saints, and attended spiritual retreats.

In June 1955 Dorothy Day and the Catholic Workers began a tradition of civil disobedience in regard to the air-raid drills that were mandated by the Civil Defense Act. The act required that all citizens take shelter for at least ten minutes while the sirens sounded during air-raid drills. Children gathered in hallways in schools, adults in cement-block shelters, waiting for the all-clear siren. The Catholic Workers would not obey the air-raid signal because they wanted to draw attention to the terrible threat the atomic bomb held over the world, and because they felt the raids lulled people into the false belief that they could survive such an attack.

For a while the workers were arrested when they did not obey the drills, and Dorothy found herself back in prison. She spent the time spreading Christ's words to other prisoners. Visiting prisoners was one "corporal work of mercy" for which she had never had much time. Now she could minister to prisoners by becoming a prisoner herself. Dorothy was arrested four times before New York City decided to stop arresting demonstrators in 1960. Eventually the drills were discontinued.

Over the ensuing years the Catholic Worker movement continued to adapt to changing times, but only in regard to the problems faced, not to the solutions. Dorothy wrote in her column in the 1960s about the Civil Rights movement and justice and equality for blacks. She had tremendous admiration for Martin Luther King Jr. and his abiding faith that men could live together as brothers. In the 1970s she joined with others to protest the Vietnam War, reminding the nation again of Christ's admonition to "love your enemies; overcome evil with good." In 1973 she joined Cesar Chavez and the United Farm Workers in California for a nonviolent demonstration against the Teamster's Union. She was arrested and jailed for ten days, her last imprisonment.

Old Catholic Workers died or left to follow other paths. New members came on to continue the work. Dorothy lamented the fact that many of the clergy were leaving the church, and the number of new priests and nuns was dwindling. Hospitality houses began facing the problems of drug abuse and illicit sex, new problems in a changing world. But Dorothy's reaction was consistent: "We reaffirm our belief in the ultimate victory of good over evil, of love over hatred, and we believe that the trials which beset us in the world today are for the perfecting of our faith."

In later years she traveled to Rome and then to India, where she met Mother Teresa. But Dorothy's health was failing, and the many years of traveling and hard work were beginning to take their toll. She died on November 29, 1980. She was eighty-three years old.

Today the work of Dorothy Day and Peter Maurin and the Catholic Worker movement continues in barrios, on city streets, and in farm communities and hospitality houses. There are over 175 independent Catholic Worker communities throughout the world that still labor to help the poor and the sick and to follow the gospels of Jesus Christ. Catholic Workers serve many people, but they are not always social workers. They follow the gospels, but they are not always members of the clergy. Although the hospitality houses and communities are independent of each other and offer varying types of services, they still offer food distribution, through both the old-fashioned soup kitchens and newer food pantries. Some of the farms run small businesses to raise funds. Some houses offer services to those addicted to drugs. Some offer social services to poor immigrants. Catholic Workers continue to protest injustice and racism and to cherish the dignity of every human being.

The *Catholic Worker* newspaper is still published and still costs only one penny, although any amount of donation is accepted and appreciated. In today's Catholic Worker one can read columns written by new voices espousing social action, but one can also find reprints of the writings of Peter Maurin and Dorothy Day, as well as a listing of the locations of hospitality houses throughout the world where their work continues.

Dorothy Day turned a life of aimless wandering and insecurity into a life of focused accomplishment. She lived the tenets of her faith even when those tenets were politically unpopular, even when she was criticized and imprisoned for them. Any doubts she might have had did not concern themselves with whether her stand was what Jesus would have wanted, but rather with herself, worrying that she was becoming too proud, "pandering to the weakness of others to build up her own feelings of holiness." Although there has been talk of canonization, she herself scoffed at the idea. "Don't call me a saint," she once said. "I don't want to be dismissed so easily."

Dorothy found her joy in community—community of church, of workers, of family. In the last lines of *The Long Loneliness*, she tells us, "We cannot love God unless we love each other, and to love we must know each other. We have all known the long loneliness and we have learned that the only solution is love, and that love comes with community. It all happened while we were sitting there talking, and it is still going on."

IBLIOGRAPHY

DEBORAH DUNCH MOODY

Cooper, Victor H. *A Dangerous Woman: New York's First Lady Liberty.* Bowie, Md.: Heritage Books, 1995.

Crawford, Deborah. *Four Women in a Violent Time.* New York: Crown Publishers, 1970.

Encyclopedia Americana. Vol. 25. New York: Grolier, 1996.

Garraty, John A., and Mark C. Carnes, eds. *American National Biography.* Vol. 15. New York: Oxford University Press, 1999.

Horton, H. P. "America's First Woman Patentee." *The Long Island Forum,* January 1945.

James, Edward T., and Janet Wilson James and Paul S. Boyer. *Notable American Women.* Vol. II. Cambridge, Mass.: Belknap Press of Harvard University Press, 1971.

Long Island, Our Story. New York: Newsday, 1998.

MacKay, Robert, ed., and Geoffrey L. Rossano and Carol Traynor. *Long Island: Between Ocean and Empire.* Cal.: Windsor Publications, 1985.

Morice, John H. "Lady Deborah Moody." *The Long Island Forum,* May 1945.

Prime, Nathaniel S. *A History of Long Island.* New York: Robert Carter, 1845.

Thompson, Benjamin F. *The History of Long Island from Its Discovery to the Present Time.* New York: Gould Banks and Co., 1843

KATERI TEKAKWITHA

Bunson, Margaret R. *Kateri Tekakwitha: Mystic of the Wilderness.* Huntington, Ind.: Our Sunday Visitor Publishing, 1992.

Daughters of St. Paul. *Blessed Kateri Tekakwitha: Mohawk Maiden.* Boston, Mass.: Daughters of St. Paul, 1980.

James, Edward, ed. *Notable American Women 1607–1950.* Vol. III. Cambridge, Mass.: Belknap Press of Harvard University, 1971.

Liguori online. www.ligouri.org.

The New Catholic Encyclopedia. Vol. II. Washington, D.C.: Catholic University, 1967.

The Position of the Historical Section of The Sacred Congregation of Rites on the Introduction of the Cause for Beatification and Canonization and on the Virtues of the Servant of God, Katharine Tekakwitha, The Lily of the Mohawks. New York: Fordham University Press. Translated in 1940.

Ruether, Rosemary Radford, and Rosemary Skinner Keller. *Women and Religion in America.* Vol. 2: *The Colonial and Revolutionary Periods.* New York: Harper & Row, 1983.

Sargent, Daniel. *Catherine Tekakwitha.* New York: Longmans, Green and Co., 1940.

Wynne, John J. *Katharine Tekakwitha: Lily of the Mohawks.* New York: The Home Press, 1922.

SYBIL LUDINGTON

Clyne, Patricia Edwards. *Patriots in Petticoats.* New York: Dodd, Mead & Co., 1976.

Congressional Record. Appendix A3168. "Remarks of Hon. R. Barry of New York at Garden Party, National Women's Party. Extension of Remarks of Hon. Robert R. Barry of New York, the House of Representatives. May 20, 1963."

Dacquino, V. T. *Sybil Ludington: The Call to Arms.* Fleischmanns, N.Y.: Purple Mountain Press, 2000.

Johnson, Willis Fletcher. *Colonel Henry Ludington: A Memoir.* Privately published by his grandchildren, Lavinia Elizabeth and Charles Henry Ludington, 1907.

Silcox-Garrett, Diane. *Heroines of the American Revolution: America's Founding Mothers.* Chapel Hill, N.C.: Green Angel Press, 1998.

Van Dusen, Albert E. *Connecticut.* New York: Random House, 1961.

Zall, P. M. *Becoming American: Young People in the Revolution.* Hamden, Conn.: Shoe String Press, 1993.

BIBLIOGRAPHY

EMMA HART WILLARD

Anticaglia, Elizabeth. *Twelve American Women.* Chicago: Nelson-Hall, 1975.

Emma Willard School online. www.emma.troy.ny.us/.

Garraty, John A., and Mark C. Carnes, eds. *American National Biography.* Vol. 23. New York: Oxford University Press, 1999.

James, Edward T., and Janet Wilson James and Paul S. Boyer. *Notable American Women.* Vol. III. Cambridge, Mass.: Belknap Press of Harvard University Press, 1971.

Lutz, Alma. Emma Willard: *Pioneer Educator of American Women.* Boston: Beacon Press, 1964.

Willard, Emma Hart. *An Address to the Public; Particularly to the Members of the Legislature of New York, Proposing a Plan for Improving Female Education.* Part of "Essential Documents in American History, 1492–Present." Compiled by Norman P. Desmaris and James H. McGovern of Providence College.

Yost, Edna. *Famous American Pioneering Women.* New York: Dodd, Mead & Co., 1961.

AMELIA JENKS BLOOMER

Bloomer, D. C. *Life and Writings of Amelia Bloomer.* Boston: Arena Publishing, 1895.

Gattey, Charles Neilson. *The Bloomer Girls.* New York: Coward-McCann, 1967.

Giele, Janet Zollinger. *Two Paths to Women's Equality.* New York: Twayne Publishers, 1995.

Gurko, Miriam. *The Ladies of Seneca Falls: The Birth of the Women's Rights Movement.* New York: Schocken Books, 1974.

National Park Service Web page. www.nps.gov/wori/gsmith.htm.

New York Times. September 18, 1851.

Ward, Geoffrey C., and Ken Burns. *Not for Ourselves Alone: The Story of Elizabeth Cady Stanton and Susan B. Anthony.* New York: Alfred A. Knopf, 1999.

HARRIET TUBMAN

Bentley, Judith. *Harriet Tubman.* New York: Franklin Watts, 1990.

Blockson, Charles L. *The Underground Railroad.* New York: Prentice Hall, 1987.

Conrad, Earl. *Harriet Tubman.* New York: Paul S. Eriksson, 1969.

Garraty, John A., and Mark C. Carnes, eds. *American National Biography.* Vol. 21. New York: Oxford University Press, 1999.

Litwack, Leon, and August Meier, eds. *Black Leaders of the Nineteenth Century.* Urbana-Champaign, Ill.: University of Illinois Press, 1988.

Smith, Jessie Carney, ed. *Notable Black American Women.* Detroit, Mich.: Gale Research, 1992.

Tobin, Jacqueline L., and Raymond G. Dobard. *Hidden in Plain View: A Secret Story of Quilts and the Underground Railroad.* New York: Anchor Books, 2000.

EMILY WARREN ROEBLING

Kass-Simon, G., and Patricia Farnes. *Women of Science: Righting the Record.* Bloomington: Indiana University Press, 1990.

Logan, Mary S. *The Part Taken by Women in American History.* New York: Arno Press, 1972. Originally published 1912.

Mann, Elizabeth. *The Brooklyn Bridge.* New York: Mikaya Press, 1996.

McCullough, David. *The Great Bridge.* New York: Simon and Schuster, 1983.

New York Times. May 23, 1883.

St. George, Judith. *The Brooklyn Bridge: They Said It Couldn't Be Built.* New York: G. P. Putnam, 1982.

Weigold, Marilyn E. *Silent Builder.* Port Washington, N.Y.: Associated Faculty Press, 1984.

KATHARINE BEMENT DAVIS

Barnes, Joseph W. "How to Raise a Family on $500 a Year," *American Heritage* (December 1981). Illustrated by Teresa Fasolino.

Carner, Lucy Perkins. *The Settlement Way in Philadelphia.* Glenside, Pa.: Beaver College, Eugenia Fuller Atwood Library, 1964.

Davis, Allen F. *Spearheads for Reform: The Social Settlements and the Progressive Movement.* New York: Oxford University Press, 1967.

Davis, Katharine Bement. *Factors in the Sex Life of Twenty-Two Hundred Women.* New York: Harper and Brothers, 1929.

————. "Why They Failed to Marry." *Harper's Magazine,* March 1928.

Fitzpatrick, Ellen. *Endless Crusade.* New York: Oxford University Press, 1990.

James, Edward T., ed. *Notable American Women 1607–1950.* Cambridge, Mass.: Belknap Press of Harvard University Press, 1971.

McCarthy, Thomas. "Katharine Bement Davis: New York's Suffragist Commissioner." www.ci.nyc.us/html.doc/html/kbd_I.html.

Moore, Rebecca Deming. *When They Were Girls.* Philadelphia: F. A. Davis Publishing, 1923.

MARY BURNETT TALBERT

Brown, Hallie Q. *Homespun Heroines.* New York: Oxford University Press, 1988.

Clup, D. W., ed. *Twentieth Century Negro Literature.* New York: Arno Press, 1969. Originally published 1902.

Heverin, Aaron T. "The Buffalo History Works: The Pan American Exposition." intotem.buffnet.net/bhw/panamex/introduction.htm.

Hine, Darlene Clark, ed. *Black Women in America: An Historical Encyclopedia.* New York: Carlson Publishing, 1993.

Leary, Thomas E., and Elizabeth C. Sholes. *Buffalo's Pan-American Exposition.* Charleston, S.C.: Arcadia Publishing, 1998.

New York World. October 15, 1922.

Smith, Jessie Carney, ed. *Notable Black American Women.* Detroit, Mich.: Gale Research, 1992.

Williams, Lillian Serece. *Strangers in the Land of Paradise: The Creation of an African-American Community in Buffalo, N.Y., 1900–1940.* Bloomington: Indiana University Press, 1999.

SARA JOSEPHINE BAKER

Baker, Sara Josephine. *Fighting for Life.* New York: Macmillan, 1939.

Garraty, John A., and Mark C. Carnes, eds. *American National Biography.* Vol. 2. New York: Oxford University Press, 1999.

James, Edward T., ed. *Notable American Women 1607–1950.* Cambridge, Mass.: Belknap Press of Harvard University Press, 1971.

Leavitt, Judith Walzer. *Typhoid Mary: Captive to the Public's Health.* Boston: Beacon Press, 1996.

Peavy, Linda, and Ursula Smith. *Women Who Changed Things.* New York: Charles Scribner, 1983.

Ptacek, Greg. *Champion for Children's Health.* Minneapolis, Minn.: Carolrhoda Books, 1994.

GERTRUDE VANDERBILT WHITNEY

Berman, Avis. *Rebels on Eighth Street: Juliana Force and the Whitney Museum of American Art.* New York: MacMillan Publishing, 1990.

Biddle, Flora Miller. *The Whitney Women and the Museum They Made.* New York: Arcade Publishing, 1999.

Block, Maxine. *Current Biography 1941.* New York: H. W. Wilson Company, 1941.

Craven, Wayne. *American Art, History and Culture.* New York: Brown and Benchmark Publishers, 1994.

Friedman, B. H. *Gertrude Vanderbilt Whitney.* New York: Doubleday, 1978.

Garraty, John A., and Mark C. Carnes, eds. *American National Biography.* New York: Oxford University Press, 1999.

Memorial Exhibition: *Gertrude Vanderbilt Whitney.* New York: Whitney Museum of Art, 1943.

New York Times. April 18, 1942.

Patterson, Jerry F. *The Vanderbilts.* New York: Harry Abrams, 1989.

DOROTHY DAY

Allaire, James, and Rosemary Broughton. *An Introduction to the Life and Spirituality of Dorothy Day.* Catholic Worker Roundtable. www.catholicworker.org/roundtable/pddintro.htm.

Catholic Worker Roundtable. www.catholicworker.org/roundtable/cwplaces.dbm.

Coles, Robert. *Dorothy Day: A Radical Devotion.* Boston, Mass.: Addison-Wesley Publishing Co., 1987.

Day, Dorothy. *The Long Loneliness.* New York: Harper and Row, 1952.

Miller, William D. *A Harsh and Dreadful Love: Dorothy Day and the Catholic Worker Movement.* New York: Liveright, 1973.

Shipman, Charles. *It Had to Be Revolution.* Ithaca, N.Y. and London: Cornell University Press, 1993.

Zwick, Mark, and Louise Zwick. "Peter Maurin, Saint and Scholar of the Catholic Worker." www.cjd.org/paper/maurin.html.

INDEX

A

American Medical Women's Association, 128

An Address to the Public; Particularly to the Members of the Legislature of New York, Proposing a Plan for Improving Female Education, 42

Anabaptist faith, 1, 4

Anthony, Susan B., 51, 57

Arthur, Chester A., 86

B

Baker, Orlando Daniel Mosher, 119

Baker, Sara Josephine
  as assistant to the health inspector, 123
  as head of New York City's Division of Child Hygiene, 119, 124
  as insurance medical examiner, 122
  as president of the American Medical Women's Association, 128
  autobiography, *Fighting for Life*, 120
  birth of, 119
  childhood of, 119–20
  death of, 128
  death of her father and brother, 120
  death of her mother and sister, 128
  decision to become a doctor, 121
  foster care program, 127
  implementation of preventive medicine, 124, 125–26
  photograph of, 117
  relationship with her Aunt Abby, 120
  retirement of, 128

Bement, Frances, 92

Bement, Rhoda Denison, 92

Bloomer, Amelia Jenks
  adoption of two children, 60
  as advocate for temperance, 51
  as deputy postmaster, 55
  as founder and editor of the newspaper *Lily*, 50
  as lecturer, 56–57
  as teacher and governess, 51
  as women's rights advocate, 54
  death of, 60
  decision to stop wearing bloomers, 59
  discovery of bloomers, 55
  elected as president of the Woman Suffrage Society, 60
  marriage to Dexter C. Bloomer, 51–52

move to Iowa, 59
move to Ohio, 58
photograph of, 49

bloomer costume, 48, 55

Bradford, Sarah, 67

Brodess, Edward, 63

Brooklyn Bridge, 76, 80–83, 86–87

Brown, Hallie Q., 107

Brown, Jenny, 119

Burnett, Carolyn Nichols, 106

Burnett, Cornelius J., 106

C

caisson disease, 83

Catholic Worker Movement, 144

Catholic Worker, 144, 152–54, 158

Chavez, Cesar, 156

Cholonec, Father, 21, 23

Christian Settlement of Caughnawaga. *See* Mission of the Saulte

Church of England, The, 3

Civil War, 73–74

Clinton, De Witt, 43

Conrad, Earl, 71

Continental Army, 27

Crisis, The, 114

D

Danbury, Connecticut, 27–28, 31

Daughters of Temperance, 56–57

Daughters of the American Revolution, 32

Davis, Katharine Bement
as advocate for the prevention of venereal disease and narcotics, 101
as commissioner of corrections, 99
as director at the World's Columbian Exposition, 93–94
as director at the College Settlement House in Philadelphia, 92
as first woman to run for statewide office, 100
as head of the parole board, 100
as head resident at St. Mary's Street College Settlement House, 94
as superintendent of New York State Reformatory for Women, 97
as teacher, 93
birth of, 92
death of, 101
education of, 92–93, 95–96
photograph of, 91
publication of study, *Factors in the Sex Life of Twenty-Two Hundred Women*, 101
trip to Bohemia, 96

work with the Rockefeller
  Bureau of Social Hygiene,
  100–101

Davis, Oscar Bill, 92

Day, Dorothy
  arrest for protesting, 146, 156
  as founder of the *Catholic
    Worker* newspaper, 144,
    152–54, 158
  as member of the United Farm
    Workers, 156
  as pacifist, 153–55
  as reporter for *The Call*, 146
  as socialist, 145–46
  autobiography, *The Long
    Loneliness*, 158
  birth of, 144
  birth of daughter, Tamar, 148
  childhood of, 144–45
  death of, 157
  discovery of Catholicism, 147
  education of, 145–46
  involvement in the Civil Rights
    movement, 156
  lover, Forster Battingham, 147
  novel, *The Eleventh Virgin*, 147
  photograph of, 149, 154
  practicing civil
    disobedience, 156
  relationship with Peter Maurin,
    150–53, 155

Day, John, 144

de Lamberville, Father Jacques,
  18, 19, 20

Douglass, Frederick, 55, 112

DuBois, W. E. B., 109, 110

Dunch, Debora, 2

Dunch, Walter, 2

E

Elizabeth I, Queen
  (of England), 3

Emma Willard School, 47

Endecott, John, 7

F

Fighting for Life, 128

Force, Juliana Reiser, 136–37

G

Garrison, William Lloyd, 57

Gravesend, 8–12
  at present, 12
  community of, 9–10
  development of, 8
  growth of, 9
  town plot, 10

Great Depression, 143, 152

Green, Harriet, 63

H

Harper's Ferry, 72–73

Harriet Tubman, 71

Hart, Samuel, 37–38

Hester Street, 136

Hinsdale, Lydia, 38

Homespun Heroines, 107

Hospitality House, 152–53

I

Iowerano, 15–16, 21

Iroquois Indians, 14–17

J

James I, King (of England), 3

Jenks, Ananias, 51

Jim Crow laws, 107, 109–10

K

Kahenta, 14

Kenhoronkwa, 14

Kieft, William, 7–8, 9

King Charles I, King
    (of England) 3, 4

King, Martin Luther Jr., 156

L

Lickley, Phebe, 78

Lily, The, 50, 54, 55, 57, 59

Little Mothers, The, 126

Long Loneliness, The, 158

Ludington, Abigail, 26

Ludington, Henry, 26, 28, 31

Ludington, Sybil
    birth and childhood of, 26
    birth of son, Henry, 32
    compared to Paul
        Revere, 30–31
    death of, 32
    legacy of, 32, 33
    marriage to Edward
        Ogden, 32
    ride of, 25, 30
    statue of, 33

Luks, George, 136

Lyon, Mary, 46

M

Mallon, Mary, 118–19

Mary Queen of Scots, 2–3

Maurin, Peter, 144, 150–52, 155

McSorley's Bar, 136

Metropolitan Museum of
    Art, 130, 132

Middlebury College, 35, 37, 40

Miller, Elizabeth Smith, 55

Mission of the Saulte, 13, 20

Mohawk Indians, 15

Mohican Indians, 7

Moody, Deborah Dunch
    arrival in Boston, 5
    as first woman known to vote
        in any election, 2, 11

as first woman to be granted a
  land patent in the American
  colonies, 2, 9
as founder of Gravesend, 2, 8
birth and childhood of, 2
birth of children, 3
death of, 12
education of, 2
journey to New Amsterdam, 6
marriage to Henry Moody, 3
residence in Salem, 5–6

Mother Teresa, 157

Mount Holyoke Female
  Seminary, 46

N

National Association for the
  Advancement of Colored
  People (NAACP), 110, 114

National Association of Colored
  Women (NACW), 108–9, 114

New Amsterdam, 6, 7

New York City Health
  Department, 118

New York City's Division of
  Child Hygiene, 119, 124

New York State Reformatory
  for Women, 97–98

O

Oberlin College, 46

P

Pan American Exposition, 103–4

Phyllis Wheatley Club, 108, 109

Puritans, 5

Q

Quakers, 11

R

Revere, Paul, 30

"Rocked in the Cradle of the
  Deep," 45

Roebling, Emily Warren
  as active member of women's
    clubs, 88
  as first person to ride across
    the Brooklyn Bridge, 76, 86
  as first woman to speak before
    the American Society for
    Civil Engineers, 86
  as overseer of the completion
    of the bridge, 83, 86
  birth of, 78
  birth of son, John, 80
  death of, 88
  engineering, 84–85
  marriage to Washington
    Roebling, 80
  move to Brooklyn Heights, 84
  plaque in honor of, 89
  photograph of, 77
  relationship to brother,
    G. K., 79
  trip to Germany, 84

Roebling, John A., 79, 80, 81–82

Roebling, Washington, 79–80,
  82, 83

Ross, Benjamin, 63

S

Satterlee, Grace, 144

Scenes from the Life of Harriet Tubman, 67

Seneca Falls Courier, 52

settlement houses, 94–95

Seward, William H., 72

slave songs, 64–65

Sloan, John, 136

smallpox epidemic, 15

Smith, Gerrit, 55, 71

Socialist Party, 145

Spanish Civil War, 153

Spirit of Flight, 141

Stanton, Elizabeth Cady, 46, 51, 53, 92

Star Chamber, The, 4

Still, William, 71

Stuyvesant, Peter, 11

T

Talbert, Mary Burnett
as assistant principal of Bethel University, 107
as child advocate, 112
as contributor to newspaper *The Crisis*, 114
as founder of the Christian Culture Congress, 109

as host to the biennial convention of the National Association of Colored Women (NACW), 109
as national director of the Anti-Lynching Crusade, 113
as president of the NACW, 110
as president of the Phyllis Wheatley Club, 109
as recipient of the Spingarn Medal, 114
as Red Cross nurse in World War I, 111
as teacher, 107
as vice president of the NAACP, 111
birth and childhood of, 106
birth of daughter, Sara, 108
death of, 114
education of, 106–7
essay in *Twentieth Century Negro Literature*, 104
marriage to William Herbert Talbert, 108
photograph of, 105
purchase and restoration of home of Frederick Douglass, 112

Teamster's Union, 156

Tekakwitha, Kateri
adoption of, 15–16
arrival at Mission of Saulte, 21–22
baptism of, 19
bout with smallpox, 15
Catholic upbringing of, 15
childhood of, 14–15
death of, 22
death of her parents, 15

healing powers of, 23
legacy of, 24
ostracism of, 18, 19–20
refusal to marry, 17, 18, 22
religious devotion of, 19
self-punishment of, 22

Terrell, Mary Church, 107

Troy Female Seminary, The, 44–45

Tryon, William (General), 26, 27, 28, 31

Tubman, Harriet
as housekeeper and laundress, 67
as public speaker, 73
as rescuer of other slaves, 67, 69–70
as Union spy, 73
birth and childhood of, 63
brain injury of, 65
childhood illness of, 63
death of, 74
escape from slavery, 66–67
involvement in the raid on Harper's Ferry, 72–73
marriage to John Tubman, 66
marriage to Nelson Davis, 74

Turner, Nat, 65

U
Underground Railroad, 71

United Farm Workers, 156

V
Vanderbilt, Alice Gwynne, 133

Vanderbilt, Cornelius, 132–33

Vanderbilt, Cornelius II, 130, 133

W
Warren, Sylvanus, 78

Washington, Booker T., 109, 110

Water Bucket, The, 52

Webb, Lucy, 51

Wells, Eunice, 39

Wells, Sylvester, 39

Western Home Visitor, 58

Whitney, Gertrude Vanderbilt
Architectural League award, 137
artistic legacy of, 141–42
as sculptor, 135, 138, 139, 141
as writer, 133–34, 135
birth of, 132
birth of children, 135
childhood of, 133
death of husband, 140
education of, 132, 134
involvement in court battle, 140
involvement in World War I, 138
marriage to Harry Payne Whitney, 134
opening of the Whitney Museum, 140
opening of the Whitney Studio Club, 138–39
portrait of, 131

Whitney Museum of American Art, 132, 140

Whitney Studio Club, 138–39

Willard, Emma Hart
  as teacher, 35, 40
  as writer, 45
  birth of, 37
  birth of son, John, 40
  childhood of, 38
  death of, 47
  death of first husband, 46
  development of her own method
    of teaching, 41–42
  education of, 39
  involvement in the women's
    movement, 46
  marriage to and divorce from
    Christopher C. Yates, 46

  marriage to John Willard, 40
  opening of The Troy Female
    Seminary, 44–45
  portrait of, 36
  proposal to legislature, 42–43

Winthrop, John, 5

Woman Suffrage Society, 60

Women's Christian Temperance, 60

Women's Medical College of the
  New York Infirmary, 121

Women's Rights Convention, 53, 92

World War II, 153

ABOUT THE AUTHOR

Antonia Petrash was born and raised in New York State and enjoys a deep and abiding interest in its history, especially the history of its extraordinary women. In addition to her writing career, she works as a librarian and archivist and manages a small local history collection on Long Island.